THE
SUPERIOR PERSON'S FIELD GUIDE TO DECEITFUL, DECEPTIVE, AND DOWNRIGHT DANGEROUS LANGUAGE

THE SUPERIOR PERSON'S
FIELD GUIDE

TO

Deceitful, Deceptive & Downright Dangerous Language

by

PETER BOWLER

illustrations by

LESLIE CABARGA

DAVID R. GODINE · *Publisher*

BOSTON

TO DI, WITH LOVE

First published in 2008 by
DAVID R. GODINE, *Publisher*
Post Office Box 450
Jaffrey, New Hampshire 03452
www.godine.com

LIBRARY OF CONGRESS
CATALOGING-IN-PUBLICATION DATA

Bowler, Peter.
The superior person's field guide to deceitful, deceptive,
& downright dangerous language / by Peter Bowler ;
illustrations by Leslie Cabarga. – 1st ed.
p.   cm.
ISBN-13: 978-1-56792-337-7
ISBN-10: 1-56792-337-2
1. English language–Euphemism–Glossaries, vocabularies, etc.
2. English language–Jargon–Glossaries, vocabularies, etc.
3. English language–Slang–Glossaries, vocabularies, etc.
4. English language–Terms and phrases. I. Title.
PE1449.B6354 2008
428.1 — dc22
2007030407

FIRST EDITION
Printed in the United States of America

America our nation has been beaten by strangers who have turned our language inside out, who have taken the clean words our fathers spoke and made them slimy and foul.

JOHN DOS PASSOS
The Big Money

Preface

IN DAYS OF YORE, people were called people. If they had a job, they might have been called staff, or even, in a particularly formal organization, personnel. If they were fired, they were fired. Now they are no longer people. They are human resources. Not human beings, but just the human kind of resource, barely distinguished from the material kind of resource. If their jobs are terminated, they are no longer fired, they are "let go." By sacking them the company is not cutting jobs but "downsizing." If, having been let go, they join the army and are killed as part of the "collateral damage" caused by "friendly fire," their bodies are brought home not in a coffin or a body bag, but in a "transit pouch."

We should be using our wonderful language as an instrument of elucidation, not as an instrument of obfuscation, evasion, and dehumanization. In his novel *1984*, George Orwell brilliantly warned the world about the spirit-sapping power of the euphemism, about the power of sweet language, in the hands of totalitarian authority, to convert the appalling to the anodyne. More than fifty years later, in an age when the all-embracing influence of the mass media lends that power an awesome platform from which it can brainwash whole populations, the world has apparently forgotten Orwell's message.

He was not the first to warn us. Over two hundred years ago, the great American Tom Paine, the father of republican democracy, wrote about the same danger. Himself the master of the political one-liner ("these are the times that try men's souls") and the author of two books that were beacons for his generation, *The Rights of Man* and *The Age of Reason*, he had a very real awareness of the power of language to change readers' perception of reality. He had a phrase for language used in this way. "Bastilles of the word," he called it.

Where are the George Orwells and the Tom Paines of our time, now that we most need them? More than ever, we need to be aware that the deceitful and deceptive use of euphemistic language can alter our realities, can deaden our moral sensitivities, can make us, almost without thinking, accept the unacceptable. Admittedly, many of the current batch of euphemisms are intrinsically ridiculous, and so we tend to be amused by them. Who has not laughed at the absurdity of saying "mission statement" instead of "objectives," or "transit station" instead of "dump"? But what about the terms "extraordinary rendition" or "enhanced interrogation techniques" instead of "torture"? There's nothing funny there.

Self-aggrandizement is a natural tendency in today's status-conscious society. Every college wants to be called a university; every worker wants to be called an operative; every dentist wants to be called a doctor; every doctor wants to be called a consulting physician. More than ever now, there is a need for a spade to be called a spade. More than ever, there is a need for plain and meaningful English.

This is a book about words that are not always what they seem. Not all are sinister weapons from the armories of totalitarian organizations; some involve little deceptions that are harmless and even entertaining. Many are examples of the laughably pretentious. But behind the absurdity lies a grave danger. So this book is something of a departure from your author's hitherto unrelentingly frivolous approach to the outer limits of language. The first three *Superior Person's Books of Words* advocated, albeit with tongue well and truly in cheek, the use of exotic words to confuse and mislead. Now I look about me and see a world where the same principle has been applied (to our lasting disadvantage) to everyday words. My little joke has turned sour.

Almost all the words in this book were plucked from my own day-to-day exposure to the media in recent years. My examples, no matter how bizarre some may seem, did not prove at all hard to find. Although there are hundreds of them in this book, these represent merely the tip of a large and menacing iceberg. And the truly terrifying thing about this is that the people who most frequently use these words are inevitably the people with the most power and the most money. In other words, they are the people most able to shape the realities and the moralities of our consciousness. By all means, be amused by the more entertaining of these euphemisms and deceptive phrases. But also, in the words of a famous film poster from a more straight-speaking time, "be afraid – be very afraid."

Finally, a caution for the eagle-eyed reader. If you notice a word dealt with herein that was also dealt with in one of my previous books, this is not an oversight on my part. I have done this deliberately, in order to deal with the word from a very different viewpoint – the exposure of the euphemistic. Mind you, in keeping with tradition, I may have included one or more deliberate errors in the technical detail of my entries, purely to test you. That is a different thing entirely.

Peter Bowler
2007

◌ A ◌

ABLE ∾ *adj*. Unable. As in such phrases as "uniquely abled." Even in the wonderland of euphemism, is it possible that a word can mean the same as its own opposite? If you doubt this, see *disability euphemisms*. Incidentally, I have seen the extraordinary word "ableism" in print, apparently indicative of an attempt to create a pejorative comparable to "racism" and "sexism," in this case to describe attitudes and policies that are unduly influenced by the level of ability or disability of an individual. Is there nothing so absurd that it will deter the language-manipulators?

ACCESSIBLE PARKING ∾ *n*. Parking spaces set aside at shopping malls and other public places for the use of handicapped drivers. These used to be called "Handicapped" or "Disabled" parking spaces. Why do we have to be so mealy-mouthed about such things? In this case the signs saying "Accessible Parking" are saying something that demonstrably holds true for *all* parking, not just parking for the handicapped. And they are saying something that is not likely to carry the desired meaning to the person for whom they are intended – the handicapped driver. Thus, the constant search for the next level of euphemism leads to a total distortion of meaning.

ACCOMMODATE, TO ∾ *v*. Not only to put someone up in lodgings for the night. When said of a female, to "accommodate" is to receive a male in sexual congress. The range of ambiguities surrounding "accommodate" make it a useful euphemism for all kinds of subjects. Thus, when a spokesperson for the Federal Reserve starts talking about "monetary policy accommodation," what is really meant is the raising of interest rates. (The tycoons who constitute "the market" are presumably simple souls and easily panicked, so it is important not to cause them undue alarm by speaking plainly.) See also *ease*. An "accommodation collar," by the way, is an arrest made for the purpose of satisfying public opinion.

ACCOUNTANT, TURF ∾ *n*. A bookmaker who takes bets on horse races. A good example of creeping credentialism. (See also *consultant*.)

ACRONYMS ∾ The use of acronyms (abbreviations consisting of the initial letters of a group of words) always tends to have a softening effect on any references to the unpleasant. This seems especially to be the case in military circles. Thus, a casual reference to "FOBS" may leave the listener unaware that what is being talked about are Fractional Orbital Bombardment Systems that can launch nuclear weapons from orbiting satellites in space. Similarly, "MIRVs" are Multiple Independently Targeted Reentry Vehicles – a "vehicle" in this case being a missile with multiple nuclear warheads. And a "CW Agent" is a Chemical Warfare Agent. (An "agent," of course, is not an agent in the usual sense of the word, but it sounds far less unpleasant than "gas" or "weapon," doesn't it? And "nerve agent" somehow doesn't sound as threatening as "poisonous gas or liquid that cripples the human central nervous system.")

ADJUSTMENT / ALIGNMENT / REALIGNMENT ∾ *n.* (Of currency values) Nice ways to talk about devaluation without using the word "devaluation." "Adjustment" is in fact now becoming the all-purpose word to use whenever an unwelcome change in some index is being made public, regardless of whether the change is a decrease (e.g., in government assistance), or an increase (e.g., in taxes).

ADJUSTMENT CENTER ∾ *n.* A solitary confinement cell in a "correctional institution."

ADULT ∾ *adj.* Sexually explicit, pornographic.

Adult

ADVENTURE ∾ *n.* (Also "venture") A war you have started, but are a little embarrassed about and therefore want to make light of.

ADVISOR ∾ *n.* If you can't secure for yourself the cachet of having the word *consultant* (q.v.) on your business card, you can always call yourself an "advisor." But what can be made of the sign I saw today on a shop window in a small rural town – "Consulting Advisors"? What do they do? No other clue whatever was provided by the signage. Are they tax consultants? Remember, this sign was not seen in a big city financial district. Are they therapists? Grief counselors? Clairvoyants? Private detectives? Employment agencies? Mothers-in-law? Apollonius of Tyana? Fearing that they might possibly be editors, I did not venture inside, so this will forever remain a mystery.

AESTHETIC PROCEDURE ∽ *n.* The cosmetic surgery that you'd like your friends to think was not a "facelift" or a "nose job," but a necessary medical intervention carried out by a fellow of the Royal College of Surgeons with a higher degree in the fine arts. Many operations seem, by the way, to have mysteriously become "procedures" in recent years, possibly because a "procedure" is not a process normally thought of as involving a knife and shedding blood.

AFFIRMATIVE ACTION ∽ *n.* Euphemism for "positive discrimination."

AGED ∽ *adj.* Ah, the many euphemisms that officialdom employs rather than just say "old"! There are no roadside signs near retirement homes saying "Old People Cross Here" or, more endearingly, "Watch Out for the Oldies." No, the signs say "Aged Pedestrians" or "Senior Citizens Cross Here" or some such platitude, patronizing in its very subservience to the notion that plain speaking could give offense. The latest one I have come across is "ageful." As a future oldie myself, I revel in the prospect of that state, and that's what I want to be called – an oldie. And I recoil with horror from the discovery that if I follow the example of certain American institutions I will be entitled to call myself "chronologically gifted" or "experientially enhanced." (See also *twilight years*.)

ALL-OUT STRATEGIC EXCHANGE ∿ *n*. Nuclear war.

ALTERNATIVE PROCLIVITY ∿ *n*. In the writing of obituaries, a delicate way of referring to the fact that there was a reason for the deceased's never having married someone of the opposite sex.

ANIMAL SAFETY OFFICER ∿ *n*. This has been sighted as an official title for a town dogcatcher.

ANTIQUES ∿ *n*. Are not always so. Signs observed by the author, hanging outside shops in his region, include:

> Antiques, New and Old
> Antiques made to Order
> We Buy Junk and Sell Antiques

APPROPRIATE TECHNOLOGY ∿ *n*. Another military and government euphemism for torture. (See also *enhanced interrogation techniques*.)

ARBORICULTURE ∿ *n*. A good example of the deceptive use of a pretentious word to describe an essentially unpretentious activity. An arboriculturalist is, put simply, a nurseryman specializing in trees, or a tree surgeon, or a pruner, lopper, or chopper of trees. But what am I to make of the advertisement that I see before me as I write this? It is in the local paper, in the section where various tradesmen and providers of practical services advertise their wares. The body of the advertisement lists "tree surgery" and "stump grinding" as the two services on offer.

But the banner headline reads "Performance Arboriculture." *Performance* arboriculture? What is this? Does the tree lopper paint his face silver, dress in a leotard, and swing backwards and forwards from a trapeze while juggling his chainsaw, with musical accompaniment on the ground from an Indonesian gamelan?

ARTILLERY ❧ *n.* The hypodermic needle and related accessories used for injections by drug addicts.

ASSEMBLY CENTER ❧ *n.* A prison, more particularly for large groups of people such as internees during wartime. A concentration camp.

ATTENDANT ❧ *n.* A term used to give illusory status to the work of one who is employed to be the servant of his employer's customers. Thus, an "air hostess" is now called a "flight attendant." Instead of "waiters" (and, happily, the abominable "waitpersons"), we now have "dining room attendants."

❧ B ❧

BACKEND ADMINISTRATION ❧ *n.* That part of the activities of an investment fund that involves communication with the fund's customers. A dismissive term, indicative of the fund's disdain for those who give it money.

BACK GATE PAROLE ❧ *n.* A death from natural causes of a prison inmate.

BAGELS ❧ *n.* Love handles, i.e., the bulging fat on some women's hips and lower abdomens.

BELL BOY ∾ *n*. Code name for a 1951 program to equip American F-89 interceptors with air-to-air nuclear weapons.

BENCHMARK ∾ *n*. A standard against which one's performance can be measured. In managerial cant, often used in conjunction with the term "best practice." When being interviewed for one of those managerial jobs in a large corporation where you get a high salary for dressing well, speaking confidently, and not managing to finish your work until well after dark, thus gaining a reputation with your bosses as a hard worker, make a point of using both terms, preferably in the one sentence. "Well, I'm a strong believer in the importance of benchmarking; without it you'll never achieve best practice."

BENIGN ∾ *adj*. Medical term meaning "not malignant." An agonizing recurrent pain – one that causes the sufferer extreme distress but that can be shown not to be caused by terminal cancer or serious cardiovascular disease – may be so described by the medical profession, though *not* by the sufferer. "Benign neglect" comes to us from a different area – that of social policy – where it refers to a conscious policy of withholding government assistance (such as welfare payments, educational support, etc.) from disadvantaged groups, as for example racial minorities, in the belief that the necessity of self-help will be more conducive to the improvement of their condition.

BIOGRAPHICAL LEVERAGE ∾ *n*. Blackmail.

BISHOP ∾ *n*. One of the innumerable slang terms (far too many to list here) for "penis." In this case, apparently derived from the similarity in shape to the bishop in a game of chess. Thus, to "bash the bishop" is one of the equally innumerable terms for "masturbation." A "Barclays," by the way, is another. (English rhyming slang – "Barclay's Bank," for "wank.")

BURN, TO ∾ *v*. To kill by electrocution, as in the electric chair.

C

CALCIFICATION ∾ *n*. A term sometimes used in the funeral business to avoid the necessity of talking to the bereaved about something as explicit as "cremation." Yet "cremation" itself was originally a term of genteel evasion, to avoid the use of "incineration." Are we doomed to be forever climbing higher and higher on a ladder of euphemism, as our sensibilities become more delicate with the passing years?

CAMILLES and DYING SWANS ∾ *n*. Medical terms for patients who loudly proclaim the imminence of their death when in fact their condition is not noticeably terminal. "Camilles" is a distortion of *camélias*, from Dumas's *La Dame aux camélias*, whose death in her operatic guise in Verdi's *La Traviata* is preceded by a certain amount of vocalization. Given the conclusion of *Rigoletto*, perhaps "Gildas" would be an even more appropriate name.

CANNED GOODS ∾ *n*. A virgin. Hardly a euphemism, but certainly a way of avoiding the necessity for plain speaking.

8

CARD-CARRYING ∾ *adj*. In the days of the McCarthy hysteria over communism, communists were always described not just as "communists" but as "card-carrying communists." Mysteriously, the term was not applied to members of other organizations, political or otherwise, who presumably also carried membership cards, and indeed there was no particular reason for the assumption that communists were obliged to carry their membership cards about with them. In these days of coffee-shop discount cards, pension cards, credit cards, and the like, everyone is card-carrying and the term has lost its pejorative overtones.

CASH FLOW EPISODE ∾ *n*. Commercial jargon normally used to imply that an approaching or imminent insolvency is merely a *challenging* (q.v.) stage in the ongoing "trading environment" of a company. Such a company may soon find itself going through a phase of "corporate recovery" – a euphemism so extreme that it means its own opposite, since it is used of a company whose affairs are being wound up by an administrator in the aftermath of a bankruptcy.

C.E. ∾ *n*. The use of "C.E." (standing for "common era") instead of "A.D." (standing for "*anno domini*") when referring to dates after the year 1 A.D. (or 1 C.E.), is a well-intentioned attempt to recognize that a large proportion of the world's population does not recognize the "dominum" in question. It does cause a certain amount of confusion, but is more likely to catch on in the long run than other equally well-intentioned linguistic reform proposals, such as Esperanto or George Bernard Shaw's revised English spelling.

CENTERS OF EXCELLENCE ∽ *n.* Institutions of
learning or research, so called to lend them an intellectual
cachet that they would not otherwise have been
able to acquire, and to give a glow
of satisfaction to those
who fund them.

CHALLENGED, CHALLENGING ∽ *adj.* Words that flag
the possible proximity of a euphemism. "Challenged" is a
common enough form to put most of us on the alert.
"Visually challenged" for blind, "physically challenged"
for crippled, "aurally challenged" for deaf, "verbally challenged" for illiterate, and so on. But "challenging" has its
own place in the lexicon of deceptive language. Did you
know, for example, that a rude and uncontrollable child
may be referred to as exhibiting "challenging behavior"?
And how many times have you heard a company chairman, giving his report on what has been a bad year for
the company, refer to the "challenging economic environment"? To be "sartorially challenged" is to be slovenly
dressed. "Inconvenienced" may also be trotted out when
"challenged" is thought to have been overdone. Thus,
"chemically inconvenienced" means
drunk or drugged.

CHICAGO PIANO ∽ *n.* A favorite of your piano-
loving, cowardly author. A Chicago piano was the Thompson machine gun favored by bootlegging gangsters in the
days of prohibition.

CHRONIC FATIGUE SYNDROME ∽ *n.* In the army,
this used to be called "LMF," i.e., "Low (or Lack of) Moral
Fiber." Then generals started coming down with it, and
it was at once seen to be a serious medical condition.

CIRCUMFERENTIALLY CHALLENGED ～ *adj*. Fat.

CLASSIFIED ～ *adj*. How did a word that means simply "categorized" come to carry also the meaning "confidential" in the world of security? Presumably because documents were at first said to be "classified as confidential/secret/top secret" (or whatever); and then the passion in the security world for ever greater security led to a hesitancy to reveal to the outside world just what precise level of security a file carried, and the realization that the single word "classified" would cover a multitude of levels and keep the outsiders at bay.

CLOSURE ～ *n*. As this book is being written, there is probably no more overused phrase in media coverage of deaths, rapes, or extreme loss of property than "closure." The victim or the bereaved is said to have a need for closure, i.e., for some sense of completion of the unhappy *incident* (q.v.) so that it can be put behind them and they can be enabled to concentrate on rebuilding their life and facing the future. This raises the whole question of clichés. Your author is heretical in this matter. He approves of clichés. A cliché is a cliché simply because it has been thought over time by a majority of people to express a particular meaning with a nice exactitude. In the present case, it is hard to think of a better term than "closure."

CO-BELLIGERENT ～ *n*. "Collaborator" has become a dirty word, since the activities of quislings in the Second World War. So when it's *our* side that is enlisting the aid of others, we call them "co-belligerents."

COLLAPSIBLE CONTAINER ～ *n*. In some states, official police term for "condom." Why are the police, of all people – tough strong-minded people all of them or they wouldn't survive in the job – seemingly so delicate in the language of their reporting? They never find a "dead man" at a crime scene; rather "a deceased male person" or "a person who has been the subject of fatal injuries." One is reminded of D. H. Lawrence's poem, written on the occasion of the police seizure of his paintings for showing naked women with pubic hair:

> Pure virginal policemen came
> And hid their faces for very shame.

With regard to police announcements at the scene of suspicious deaths, this author advocates the revival of the word "perish." Instead of telling the media that "there is a deceased male person at the scene," the police spokesman would say "a young man perished here tonight." By the way, how can a death be suspicious? Only people can be suspicious. A death should surely be described as "suspicion-engendering."

COLLATERAL DAMAGE ✤ *n.* Once this meant damage caused by fire, flood, theft, or storm to uninsured goods kept as security for a loan. Now it means the killing of innocent civilians in war. For example, the deaths of schoolchildren as an unintended spin-off to a bombing raid or a shelling bombardment. Or perhaps the result of a bomber unloading its explosive cargo on a "target of opportunity" (a euphemism, since the Second World War, for the more or less random release of bombs on the way back from a raid that failed to find its intended target).

COMMISSION ✤ *n.* In the world of financial management advising, a bribe paid to the advisor to sell a product to a client. Also known, even more euphemistically, as a "sweetener" – or, as the French put it, a "*douceur*."

COMMISSIONAIRE ∾ *n*. A doorman.

COMMUNITY-ALIENATED ∾ *adj*. Criminal.

CONDUCT OUR OPERATIONS, TO ∾ *v*. To bomb and shell areas where civilian men, women, and children are living. From an Israeli spokesman's reference to his government's intention to continue to "conduct our operations" against areas of Lebanon.

Collateral Damage

CONSCRIPTION ∾ *n*. Nowadays called anything but conscription, to minimize in the public mind the evident unjustness of the process. Instead, it's "national service" ("national" being a word with good connotations) or "the draft" (a word that is at least neutral in its connotations).

CONSENSUS ∾ *n*. No, *not* spelled "concensus." And *not* meaning "majority agreement." It means "*everyone* agreeing." At the end of a heated and inconclusive debate about the motion you have put forward at the school's parents and teachers meeting, you could sweetly ask your main antagonist: "Well, let's compromise here. Let's not ask the secretary to record an actual majority in favor, but, since you disagree with the idea, just leave it on the basis that she record it as a general consensus." With any luck he will go along with this, and won't find out until three meetings later what "consensus" really means.

CONSTRUCT ❧ *n.* When used as a noun by an academic author, a meaningless word. (See also *structure*.)

CONSULTANT ❧ *n.* A word that used to mean "someone who consults." Now used in job titles and on business cards as a generic term meaning little more than "employee." In the areas of real estate, and of product and services selling, we used to have "salesmen" and "saleswomen." Now they have been transmogrified into "sales consultants." But do they consult? No, they sell. This is a classic example of credentialism, i.e., the natural tendency of humankind to aggrandize the status of their institution, their employer, or their occupation. The security officers who frisk you at airports or patrol shopping malls now carry not only guns, but also business cards saying "security consultant." I have even heard of mercenary soldiers, the kind that are recruited to invade small African provinces, being referred to as "defense consultants." I would bet good money, if I had any, on the inevitability that in due course the men who drive the trash collecting truck will become "resource recovery consultants."

COORDINATOR ❧ *n.* A "coordinator" can, and does, do all those things that a "consultant" can do, without ever having to coordinate anything. He can be a "sales coordinator," i.e., a salesman, or a "health and fitness coordinator," i.e., a gym attendant, or a "facility admission coordinator," i.e., a doorman.

CORRECTION OFFICER ∾ *n.* No, not an editor, proof-reader, or classroom teacher, but a prison warden. What was I saying about credentialism?

COST REDUCTIONS ∾ *n.* Job cuts. Only the other day I heard this one from a big business CEO who, when asked by a TV interviewer if his firm was planning job losses, replied entirely in terms of "cost reductions" and never once mentioned the word "jobs." (If "cost reductions" is thought by the euphemizer to be unduly meaningful, he may resort to talking about "resource re-allocation.")

COUNTER-CULTURE PEOPLE ∾ *n.* No, not a movement within the postmodern intelligentsia aimed at achieving culture change in society. Rather the latest euphemism for the homeless, or street people.

COUNTER-VALUE CAPABILITY ∾ *n.* The capacity to strike only civilian targets in a nuclear bombing raid. What is the need for such a word?

CREATIVE ∾ *adj.* Deceptive and deceitful, as in "creative accounting."

CREDIBILITY ∾ *n.* The new word for truth. To modernize those famous words of Keats: "beauty is credibility, credibility beauty; that is all ye know on earth, and all ye need to know." Today, of course, credibility must have another quality besides beauty – it must have *deniability* (q.v.). Otherwise there would be no "fall-back position" in the event of a "credibility gap" being seen to have developed. Oh, and it must have "sustainability" also.

CRITICAL POWER EXCURSION ∾ *n*. Not an excursion that you'd want to go on. A meltdown at a nuclear power station.

CUSTODIAL SENTENCE ∾ *n*. No, not a combination of words containing a subject and a predicate and having a guardianship function. Just a term in prison.

CUT-AND-PASTE JOB ∾ *n*. Mild enough as a word processing function your author, in a state of demented confusion, carries out every day. But also used (behind closed hospital common room doors) by surgeons to describe an operation that had to be cut short because, on opening up the patient, the operating surgeon could see that there was no hope of effective intervention and all that could be done was to sew the patient up again.

∾ D ∾

DEATH, EUPHEMISMS FOR ∾ "Passed on." "No longer with us." "Gone to a better place." "Handed in his cards." "Gone to meet his maker." "Negative patient care outcome." "In the RAF," "Old Newton got him" (i.e., gravity brought him down to earth). A comprehensive list would be endless, and therefore I go no further. (But for the ultimate death euphemism, see *life*.)

DECIMATE, TO ∾ *v*. For the information of journalists and for all radio and TV presenters: to "decimate" a group of people or things does not mean to kill, destroy, ravage, defeat, or lay waste all or most of that group. This all-too-common usage is a classic example of the mistake that can be made by learning the meaning of a word solely from the context in which it is first encountered, and not from the dictionary. To decimate is to kill, destroy, or otherwise remove from the scene *one in every ten* of the members of that group. Get it right!

DECONTAMINATE, TO ∾ *v.* To embalm. A word from the mortuary. (Alternatively, to *massage* [q.v.] the content of a document in order to *sanitize* [q.v.] it for public consumption.)

DEEP INTERROGATION ∾ *n.* Torture.

DEFENCE/DEFENSE ∾ *n.* War, including preemptive attack. A military term. In an earlier and simpler age the U.K. Ministry of Defence used to be called the War Office.

DEFENSIVE VICTORY ∾ *n.* A defeat that can be presented to the defeated troops as a planned retreat in accordance with strategic objectives. A retreat may also be described as a "stratagem to draw the enemy into a trap," a "withdrawal to prepared positions," or "a shortening of the front line."

DEFERRED SUCCESS ∾ *n.* Would you believe "failure"? A term from the magic land of modern education. The latest attempt to spare the unsuccessful the shame of being seen as unsuccessful.

DENIABILITY ∾ *n.* A characteristic of political statements that permits them to be wriggled out of at some later stage. A word that has somehow emerged from the

dark crevices of clandestine propaganda campaign planning within which, for obvious reasons, it had previously
been confined, and is now exposed, like a worm stranded
by retreating rainwater, to the sunlight of the outside
world. Deniability, of course, should have *credibility* (q.v.).

DENIAL, IN ∿ *adj*. Another extremely popular cliché
at the present time (or "now," as we used to say). A person is said to be in denial if he fails to admit some truth
about himself, and moreover fails to admit that he fails to
admit it. Normally said about someone with whom you
disagree, being a much more patronizing way to express
your disagreement, conveying as it does not only that the
other person is wrong, but also that he has a
pitiable psychological defect.

DEVELOPMENT CASE ∿ *n*. A student of inferior academic ability who gains admission to a U.S. college because
the college stands to gain financially from enrolling the student. In the world of academia, by the way, a "development
officer" is a fund-raiser. (See also *legacy*.)

DEVELOPMENTALLY CHALLENGED ∿ *adj*. (Also
"developmentally different") Below average in intelligence. Slow on the uptake. Sadly, there seem to be a particularly colorful variety of expressions, sometimes quite
confusing, intended to convey this sense. "Special." "Excep-
tional." "Acceptional" (*sic*). "Lesser (*sic*) developed." A
"mouth breather" is just a dullard. As is someone who is
"camping with the clan of the dimly lit," or "thin in the
crust." Or someone of whom it can be said that "the
lights are on but there's no one home." But someone who
is "out where the buses don't run" may be not only dull
but also out of touch with reality to the extent that they

are given to wild fancies. Much the same as someone who "doesn't have both oars in the water."

DIGITAL TERRESTRIAL RECEIVER ∾ *n*. What could this be, do you think? It sounds as though it might be an advanced communications device on a spaceship, returning to planet Earth from the Orion constellation by homing in on a terrestrial signal. Well, no; it's a name observed by the author on what used to be called, with remarkable clarity, a set-top box, i.e., the device that you connect to your old analog TV to enable it to receive digital telecasts.

DISABILITY EUPHEMISMS ∾ Question: when is a word its own opposite? Answer: when it's a twenty-first-century euphemism. In this case, for "able," read "disabled." The disabled are now called "differently abled" or "uniquely abled." The disabled may even be called "differently advantaged." This general area is a major sub-category of deceptive and confusing language. The blind may be called "non-sighted," "optically challenged," "sight deprived," or "experiencing visual deficit." The deaf may be "aurally challenged," "hearing-impaired," or "hard of hearing." A group whose test results are lower than most groups are called "disparately impacted," a descriptive that is thought to justify the *massaging* (q.v.) of their test scores. In the U.K., antidiscrimination regulations are worded in such a way that, according to a government survey, as much as 25 percent of the adult population could fit the definition of disabled. (For another example of a word that is its own opposite, see *life*.)

DISASSEMBLE, TO ∾ *v*. According to the person who, as I write this, is president of the United States, a position thought to require significant cognitive skills, this means "dissemble." Heard him say it myself, *live* (q.v.) on TV, 1 June 2005.

DISINFLATION ∾ *n*. Politician's word for a mild recession in the national economy. After all, if "inflation" is bad, "disinflation" must be good, mustn't it?

DISPERSAL ∾ *n*. In case you think that the reality-altering euphemism is a device of our own times, be aware that in nineteenth-century Queensland (Australia's Florida), the "Dispersal Programme" was the name given to a government policy that was expected to lead to the eventual extermination of the indigenous population.

DISTURBED ∾ *adj*. A person whose statements or behavior does not accord with your own may be so described if you are unable to come up with any factual or logical objections to what he is saying or doing. Also a euphemism for children who misbehave.
(See also *maladjusted*.)

DOUBLE-ENTRY ACCOUNTING ∾ *n*. Originally, double-entry bookkeeping was simply a technique to double-check the correctness of accounts and ensure their security from loss or theft. Before long, it became a technique to evade tax by keeping two different sets of accounts, one for public (and the tax collector's) consumption and the other the genuine set. Now there is "triple-entry accounting," and given the ingenuity of the accounting profession, the sky's the limit.

DOWNSIZE, TO ∾ *v*. Well, we all must know by now what this one means. One of the first of the modern managerial euphemisms. When your company is firing staff, to describe the process as downsizing implies that no human beings are involved in any way, let alone that any are actually being disadvantaged. The latter-day Euphues who thought this one up bears a heavy responsibility for all those managerial evasion words that were to follow.

Downsize

DUMB ∾ *adj.* (Also "dirty," "smart," and "intelligent") All words used, believe it or not, to describe bombs. The implication is that these things are not in any way harmful, just rather cute little things with human characteristics. (See also *low-yield nuclear weapons*.) A nuclear bomb that disperses greater or lesser amounts of radioactivity may be described as "clean," depending on whether the aim is to leave buildings unharmed while killing as many people as possible, or to destroy as many buildings as possible without leaving undue levels of radioactivity, so that troops can enter the area soon afterwards. (I have seen this term used in both senses, even though they are totally opposite in meaning.) The term "nuclear bomb" is itself less alarming than its predecessor "atomic bomb," since "atomic" had come to mean "enormously big and powerful" in the popular mind, whereas everyone knows that nuclei are tiny little things.

DYSFUNCTIONAL CONFLICT PROCESSES ∾ *n*. Arguments.

DYSPHEMISM ∾ *n*. I suppose there ought to be an opposite to "euphemism," and "dysphemism" would seem to fill the bill, i.e., a term or phrase used pejoratively to reflect badly on something or someone without actual distortion of the facts. It may say something about our present-day society that examples are harder to find than examples of euphemisms. We are, it seems, much more inclined to make things seem better than they are than to make them seem worse than they are. Perhaps it would be dysphemistic to call someone an "animal" during an argument, thereby maintaining strict biological accuracy while implying that your adversary is less than human. The term "negative taxation," invented as an alternative for "income support" or "welfare payment," might be seen as a dysphemism, using as it does two extremely negative words to describe a positive thing. In the hands of the unthinking, a dysphemism, in its more general sense of any demeaning assertion, may be unintentionally absurd: recently I heard a senator, in expressing his concern at the state of the nation's literacy skills, complain that "half the population is below average." A completely different type of dysphemism, perhaps, is the use of a pejorative term without any intention to demean. Thus, a "headhunter" in modern society is not a decapitating cannibal, but some- one who specializes in finding suitable candidates to fill the senior vacancies in corporations. Perhaps this usage derives from the ever-present awareness that in due course many of the recruited heads will roll.

E

EASE, CHAPEL OF ~ *n.* The chapel at a mortuary where a short service may be held for the "departed." Also known as a "chapel of rest." Oddly enough, "chapel of ease" has also had some currency as a euphemism for a lavatory.

EASE, TO ~ *v.* In the end-of-trading media reports on the stock market, have you noticed that if the market has fallen on the day, it is said to have "eased"? Much more soothing to the investors. A "technical adjustment" also means a fall in the market. Similarly, if the "job market has softened," this means that unemployment is increasing and jobs are harder to find.

EASEFUL ~ *n.* U.S. Army code word for the secret underground placement of eighty caches of arms in Austria, immediately after Word War II, to equip resistance fighters in the event of a Russian invasion.

ECDYSIAST ~ *n.* A striptease dancer. From the term "ecdysis," a zoological term for the act of casting off an integument, or outer covering, as for example a snake's casting off its skin. Interestingly, "ecdysiast" is a word invented by an individual to meet a specific request – in this case H. L. Mencken had been asked by the striptease dancer Georgia Southern to come up with a classier name for her act.

Ecdysiast

ECONOMICALLY INACTIVE ∾ *adj.* Unemployed. A lesser form of unemployment is underemployment, i.e., being retained on your wage or salary but having no useful work to do. Such staff may be given the task of "writing the company's history" and are described as "sitting by the window."

EDUCATION ∾ *n.* Education used to be about "teaching," "learning," "explanation," "understanding," and such things. It is now about such things as "performativity" and "linear professional learning." It has generated perhaps more pretentious gobbledegook than any other area of human activity. Students, staff, and research workers are "embedded" in "learning environments," where they are "incentivized." What used to be called "subject masters" or "subject mistresses" are now called "discipline convenors" or "domain leaders." Teachers who undertake what used to be called "in-service training" now undertake "upskilling." Librarians are now called "information specialists" or "resource managers." Every statement of education planning includes at some point the word "strategic"; there are "strategic partnerships," "strategic issues," "strategic initiatives," "strategic developments," even "strategic pillars." And what on earth is "longitudinal information"?

EFFICIENCY GAINS ∾ *n*. Budget cuts. Term invented by government accountants whose overriding imperative is to spend less. For them, the ultimate efficiency gain would be to spend nothing at all. Except, of course, on their own salaries. Also known as "efficiency dividends." A variant is "productivity gains," which normally means mass firings.

EFFLUENT ∾ *n*. Strictly speaking, anything flowing out of something. But in the world of euphemism, a term now used to soften the impact of something really nasty, as for instance, sewage or industrial pollution.

ELECTRIC CURE ∾ *n*. Execution in the electric chair.

EMBEDDED ∾ *adj*. Official term for war correspondents placed within army units, ostensibly for their greater protection but actually for their closer supervision.

ENCOUNTER ∾ *n*. Military euphemism for "battle" or "fight." Likewise "engagement." An aerial combat between fighter planes used to be called, with great simplicity and descriptiveness, a "dogfight." It is now called an "air-to-air encounter" or, even more lovingly, an "air-to-air engagement."

ENERGY RELEASE ∾ *n*. No, not the explosive release of pent-up power that occurs at the start of the Olympic

100-meter sprint, but radiation released by a nuclear reactor. The beauty in this euphemism for those who adopted it is that it contains absolutely no reference to the radioactivity in question.

ENGINEER ∾ *n*. This looks like one to beware of in the future. It still holds true, in the main, that anyone called an "engineer" has completed a reasonably demanding course of education and training and is able to deal with such things as the impact of forces, the strength of materials, and so on. At the very least, one would expect persons calling themselves engineers to have some understanding of the operational mechanics of some engines. But there are, just beginning to creep into the language, the occasional instances of "engineer" being used simply to add prestige to the description of an otherwise undemanding job. A "sanitation engineer" is a trash collector. I have heard it said that in the U.S. Senate the shoe-shine man is now called a "footwear maintenance engineer." I assume that this is one of those jolly little jokes that senators are famous for the world over, but I am less confident about the intention behind the job title "pool maintenance engineer." There is a real danger that "engineer" will become tomorrow's *consultant* (q.v.) or *coordinator* (q.v.). As may its fellow term "technician." We already are quite used to "beauty technician" or its compressed form "beautician" for a hairdresser, words that would have engendered much scorn and derisive laughter as recently as seventy-five years ago but are now, God help us, part of the language. As for "aesthetician," words, you will be relieved to hear, fail me.

ENHANCED INTERROGATION TECHNIQUES ∾ *n*. Torture. Deprivation of sleep. Deprivation of capacity to

26

move. Being secured to a board sloping so that the head is downwards and having water poured into the nostrils. Being compelled to participate in a "Bell Telephone Hour," in which the wires of an army field telephone are put to a non-telephonic use. (And, if that doesn't work. . . See *extraordinary rendition*.) The use of "enhanced" is a particularly insidious piece of deception, since it is a word that ordinarily suggests positive connotations that are all good. "Enhanced" normally means "bettered" or "improved," as in "community members will have enhanced lifestyle opportunities with the building of this new center." The Reagan administration at one point started talking about taxes as "income enhancement." More recently, a Texan member of the House of Representatives proposed a measure called "The Terrorist Death Penalty Enhancement Act," which was intended to increase the variety of crimes that would incur the death penalty. And an "enhanced radiation weapon" is not one that you'd want to get to know too closely.

ENHANCED OFFERING ∾ *n.* Another example of the insidious power of "enhanced" to sugarcoat an otherwise unpleasant pill. The publishers of already-ultra-expensive textbooks often market their new editions as "enhanced offerings," that is to say bundled with instructional supplements such as a CD-ROM and/or an online service requiring registration – all of which enables the publishers to charge even more for the textbooks. And how often is "system enhancement," referring to a claimed improvement in a firm's computing hardware or software, used as a justification for a mistake or even a catastrophic failure of a service? A case coming to notice recently was that of a superannuation fund failing to make a necessary update to a client's entitlements and then excusing itself by saying that this "was due to a system enhancement."

27

ENTERTAINMENT, CORPORATE ∾ *n*. Bribery.

EPISODE ∾ *n*. If your doctor uses this one, "Well, old chap, it seems that you have had an episode of. . . ," be very afraid. Another episode, and you'll be getting towards the end of the serial. You should also be worried if he starts talking about an *incident* (q.v.).

EQUITY RETREAT ∾ *n*. A fall on the stock market. (See also *ease*.)

ERGONOMIST ∾ *n*. Not quite the same as its now rather outdated predecessor "time-and-motion expert," since ergonomists focus in particular on the physical impact on staff of their work situation, whereas time-and-motion experts were somewhat callous efficiency experts whose only concern was the maximization of productivity and profit through the speeding up of procedures. Nowadays, of course, corporations' only concern is for the health and well-being of their workers (sorry – operatives), and the profit motive is relegated to secondary status.

ESTATE CONDITION ∾ *n*. An auctioneer's euphemism, intended to conceal from likely bidders that the deceased person's belongings being auctioned are not in the best of condition. In this case, the "estate" (being a "deceased estate") carries a rather different significance than it does in *real estate* (q.v.), generally.

ETHICAL INVESTMENT ∾ *n*. A relatively new term, indicative of an emerging trend for fund managers to seek to exploit the socially concerned and "green" segment of the investing public. The theory is that an ethical investment fund will not invest in, for example, the arms industry. Does this mean that Victory Bonds were unethical during the Second World War? For that matter, is investment itself, the aim of which is to make more money, an ethical activity? What is it that Jesus was reported to have said about the eye of a needle?

ETHICIST ∞ *n*. One who is employed, assigned, or commissioned by a university, a government agency, a corporation – even, amazingly, by the military – to advise on the ethical aspects and repercussions of its activities. The relatively recent emergence of ethicism as a specialist profession is perhaps the most powerful indication of the depths of moral bankruptcy to which our society has sunk. The implication is that people who are not professional ethicists cannot, and – even more worryingly – need not, concern themselves with ethical issues. By employing an ethicist (and even, perhaps, supporting him or her with an ethics committee), the president and the chief executive officer of the corporation effectively distance themselves from the moral responsibilities of the corporation. In today's paper, in the Positions Vacant section, I see that there is an advertisement for a "hospital ethicist." The hospital in question is a Catholic hospital. Will the next step perhaps be to advertise for a "church ethicist"? Another advertisement seen recently, for a promotions officer for a large firm, included the phrase "flexible work ethic required."

EXCHANGE OF VIEWS ∞ *n*. Diplomacy-speak for "complete disagreement." The exchange may have been "full and frank" or "cordial"; makes no difference; when we see the phrase "exchange of views" we know that this has been a knockdown, dragout fight, and that it hasn't finished yet.

EXTRAORDINARY RENDITION ∾ *n*. No, not one of your author's infamous poetry readings. This is a term used by the U.S. military for the process whereby a captive is stripped of his clothes, dressed in a bright orange jumpsuit, has his hands and legs shackled, is blindfolded or simply head-bagged, and is placed on a Gulfstream V jet to be flown like a sack of potatoes to Egypt to be tortured.

∾ F ∾

FACILITATOR ∾ *n*. Someone who can't do something, hired for good money to orchestrate an attempt to enable others to do it. When companies send their junior executives off to a "personal development" seminar, why can't they just call the course-giver a "teacher"? Why this pretense that those attending the course will discover things for themselves, with a little help from a process-organizer? (When, fifty and more years ago, educationists were promoting the "discovery method" as the best way for schoolchildren to learn, why did they not allow their student teachers to discover the discovery method for themselves?) The classic arena for the "facilitator," of course, has been that of "total quality management," a fashionable system under which a corporation is given an enormous amount of paperwork to complete, with the intent that all its processes will then become entirely foolproof. And hence effective in corporations staffed by fools.

FACILITY ∾ *n*. Once this word meant simply "ease," in the sense of the easiness with which something is done. "She showed great facility in her execution of the difficult octave passages." Now, facility has become a *thing*. A facility can be an object, a machine, a building, an appliance, a service, a bank loan – almost anything. I am keying these words into a word processing facility, and later in the day I will use a transport facility to enable me to visit my nearest retail facility. In the U.S. Army, I am told that what used to be called "mess halls" are now called "dining facilities." (In the British army, the same change has led to the existence of "regimental restaurants.") A washroom is now an "ablutions facility." Guantanamo Bay is not a prison, it is a "detention facility." Yesterday I saw a sign outside a complex of buildings declaring that it was a "Retirement and Aged Care Facility." What has happened to our language, that we can call an old people's home a retirement and aged care facility?

FADED GIANT ∾ *n*. U.S. Civil Defense code name for a plan to deal with the aftermath of any major accident in a nuclear reactor.

FAILED TO WIN ∾ *v*. A nice way of admitting that you have lost without admitting that you have lost.

FAITH-IMPAIRED ∾ *adj*. Term increasingly used by some of the gentler evangelical Christian groups to describe those who are atheistic or agnostic.
Nicely patronizing.

FAST-TRACK, TO ∾ *v*. Commonly said of a procedure that can be applied to an "option." Current cant for giving priority to something. One method of fast-tracking an option is to slow-track all the other options.

FELL OUT OF BED ∾ *v*. Failed completely and unexpectedly (said of a business enterprise).

FIELD ASSOCIATE ∾ *n.* In the U.S., a plainclothes police officer whose "mission" (see *mission statement*) is to keep an eye on the activities of other police officers in the field and report any observed corruption or other "conduct unbecoming."

FIRING, EUPHEMISMS FOR ∾ "Letting you go," "downsizing," "rightsizing," "rationalizing," "sacking," "streamlining," "beaching," "benching," "reducing your commitments." Being "selected out." Being "written out of the script," or "impacted by a reduction-in-force program." Perhaps the most chillingly euphemistic is "outplacing." To be almost fired, or set up for imminent firing, is to be "given new responsibilities." When the blow finally falls, you may say that you are "looking after your other interests."

FIRST-STRIKE CAPABILITY ∾ *n.* The capacity for a country to launch a nuclear attack on another without the latter's prior awareness. Note once more (see *energy release*) the absence of the word "nuclear."

FIXED MULTI-LINE VOICE SERVICES ∾ *n.* Telephones.

FLEXIBILITY ∾ *n.* When you hear a corporation or a government department talking about the need for greater "flexibility," be on your guard. The probability is that a total abandonment of some underlying principle is being contemplated.

FRAGMENTATION DEVICE ∾ *n.* Hand grenade.

FREE ∾ *adj.* For a price. The most egregious example of straight-out lying in the world of human relations is that of the envelope that turns up in your mail offering you something that is described, in big gold letters, as "Free!" On opening the envelope and reading the contents, you discover that the only way you can obtain this "free" gift is to buy something else. The "free" gift is therefore not free, and the people who sent this letter to you are liars. Write and tell them so. Redeem the use of the wonderful word "free"! Do not let it become its own antonym.

Friendly Fire

FRIENDLY FIRE ∾ *n.* A much-criticized military term for incidents in which you inadvertently shoot at, or bomb, some of your own people, presumably by accident. Certainly, "friendly" is stretching it a bit, isn't it? But what else could you call it, if confined to two words (in itself an admirable objective)? A variant, the very particularity of which somehow makes the term seem even more absurd, is "friendly grenade." "Blue on blue" also means bombing or shelling your own soldiers.

FROLIC ∾ *n.* Code name for a plan developed by the U.S. Strategic Air Command, in the early days of the Cold War, for nuclear war with the Soviet Union.

FRONT BURNER ∾ *n.* A term used in electronic communications to draw special attention to any *incident* (q.v.) that might result in war. If the war in question was likely to be nuclear, the code word to be used was the more immediately meaningful "Nucflash."

FULSOME ∾ *adj.* Does *not* mean just "full." The author recently heard a senior general in the armed forces – a man of much intelligence and clarity of thought, by the way – talk about a "fulsome response to a military emergency." "Fulsome" is one of those interesting cases where a pejorative overtone is added to an otherwise inoffensive word. Something, such as praise, is fulsome if it is off-putting because of its very excessiveness.

FUND-RAISING ∾ *n.* An activity that attracts euphemisms as the proverbial honey pot attracts bees. Institutions such as universities do not have fund-raising departments; they have "resource development" departments. They do not have fund-raisers; they have "development officers."

∾ **G** ∾

GARDEN CRYPT ∾ *n.* Another of those wonderful words from the American mortuary business. My source describes it as "a drawer facing outward in a store for corpses." But how can this be? What kind of a drawer would face *inward*?

GENERAL DISCHARGE ～ *n.* The alternative to an "honorable discharge" from the armed forces. In other words, this is the official euphemism for a dishonorable discharge.

GENITAL SENSATE FOCUSING ～ *n.* Would you believe . . . masturbation?

GOLD-BRICK, TO ～ *v.* To shirk hard work; to avoid one's responsibilities. Thought to have originated in the army, as for example in the case of the inventively minded private who absents himself from parades for the day through the simple expedient of carrying a trash bin around camp and, if asked by an officer what he is doing, replies smartly: "Trash detail, sir!"

GOLDEN HANDSHAKE ～ *n.* Those of us outside the senior echelons of the corporate world can be forgiven if we see entry to those echelons as comparable to entry to Aladdin's cave, since there are so many different "golden" payments you may receive, over and above what you get for doing the job. You may be given a "golden greeting" to persuade you to join a firm, a "golden handshake" to persuade you to leave it, "golden handcuffs" to induce you to remain in it, a "golden parachute" to soften your fall from an executive height, or even a "golden retriever" to get you to rejoin a firm that you have left. If you were an officer in the British army and surplus to requirements you may have been given a "golden bowler" (i.e., bowler hat) to help you on your way.

GOVERNMENTALITY ～ *n.* I have seen this word in print without being able to work out from the context what it was intended to mean. The "quality of government," perhaps? A "government instrumentality," perhaps?

Come to think of it, how did an "instrument" become an "instrumentality"? (See *infestate*.)

GRANULATE, TO ∾ *v*. To break something – say, a proposed action or policy – down into its component parts so as to examine it in more detail. A current favorite in the corporate world. Entails, of course, the risk of "not seeing the wood for the trees" – a commendable cliché that has stood the test of time and is likely to remain in currency long after "granulate" has been forgotten.

GRASS ∾ *n*. The pubic hair of a female. Also, for males as well, "short hairs," or "the short and curlies."

GROWN TALL ∾ *n*. Code name for a contingency plan for the Marine Corps to assist the army in suppressing civil unrest within the U.S.

∾ H ∾

HANDLE THE TRUTH, TO ∾ *v*. In effect, to manhandle the truth, i.e., to *massage* (q.v.) it.

HANGING, TO DIE BY ∾ *v*. This form of execution ("execution" being itself a euphemism – see *kill*) seems to have been especially fruitful of euphemisms. (The word "fruit" at once brings to mind the blues song "Strange Fruit," about the bodies of black men hanging in the trees where they were lynched.) Many of these euphemisms demonstrate a quality of rough, if macabre, humor. Being "strung up" is the first that comes to mind, and probably the commonest. But the unfortunate victim could also find himself "doing the midair dance," being the special guest at a "necktie party," "having throat trouble," "decorating a cottonwood tree," or having "hemp fever."

HARDWARE ∽ *n*. Military armament. Also, in the case of the present author's *word processing* (q.v.) *facility* (q.v.), those components too heavy to be carried and too mysterious to be subject to successful *self-assembly* (q.v.) after a house move.

HARSH INTERROGATION TECHNIQUES ∽ *n*. Torture.

HAVE A GOOD DAY/AFTERNOON/WEEKEND ∽ *phr*. Expression of sickening familiarity addressed to you at the checkout counter, the reception desk, etc. by a complete stranger, often a young person with a metal stud embedded in her lower lip. Why am I so repelled by this apparently harmless and friendly act of well-wishing? An acquaintance of mine, sadly no longer with us, a dear old lady of impeccable courtesy but strong views about modern society, invariably responded with a polite "Thank you, but I have made other arrangements." A variant of the "have a good day" farewell is the corresponding shop assistant's greeting: "How's your day been?" This seems to me to be even more intrusive into your privacy. The recommended response is in fact to *answer* the question. I mean *genuinely* answer. Inform the so-solicitous enquirer about the problem you had on getting up in finding your slippers, the sad discovery that there was no milk left in the fridge for your breakfast, the unexpected pleasure in finding that the front door lock was working again, the satisfaction you experienced in being able to park your car exactly where you wanted to . . . and so forth. By the time you are finished the shop assistant in question may be starting to have second thoughts about asking the question again of a complete stranger. And why must the strangers who deal with us in commercial transactions insist on calling us by our first name? And give us only *their* first name? Well, we know the answer to the latter question, don't we? By giving us only their first name, especially when they are dealing with us by phone, they are effectively reducing the chance of our being able to pin on them whatever bad consequences might ensue from our interaction with them. It's the modern "not my responsibility" syndrome.

HEAVY LANDING ∾ *n.* Crash landing (of an airplane). Also said to be an "off-airport landing."

Help

HELP ∾ *n.* A computer program designed to confuse users and withhold necessary information from them.

HELP, THE ∾ *n.* The servant, or servants – but we mustn't call them that, since the supplying of a service is now thought to be a demeaning function. This holds good also in the wider world outside that of domestic service.

Thus, in large corporations and government departments, what used to be called "management services" divisions (i.e., the people who oiled the housekeeping wheels for the organization in question) are now called "management divisions" (the implication being that they are the ones who call the tune).

HIGH FOREHEAD, TO HAVE A ∾ *v*. To be bald.

HOLIDAY OWNERSHIP ∾ *n*. A recently introduced replacement term for "time sharing," intended to soften the increasingly dubious reputation of the latter by highlighting the two activities thought most likely to attract investors – holidaying and owning.

HOLISTIC ∾ *adj*. Strictly speaking – and in matters philological you would surely not expect your author to speak in any other way – this derives from "holism," the philosophical theory that nature has a tendency to organize individual units into organized wholes. Do try to use it in this sense, not in the fashionable sense encountered in the area of unconventional medicine, where "holistic" treatment of a complaint may involve not only the administration of a medicinal substance, but also a "helicopter audit" (see *loop*) of the patient's diet, lifestyle, psychological condition, etc., etc. But – "holistic *dentistry*" (a sign observed by the author outside a suburban dental clinic)?

HOLY FRIAR ∾ *n*. Liar. Rhyming slang constitutes in itself a major subsection of euphemism, since most instances of rhyming slang have the effect of damping down the harshness of the term being so coyly curtained off. Some, as in the present case, go even further than that by converting a vice to a virtue.

HOME ECONOMICS ⤷ *n*. Just to show that ideological euphemism is not a purely present-day invention, let me remind you that as long as fifty or more years ago schools had stopped calling their classes for girl students "Cooking and Sewing," and had started bestowing on them the impressive, and seemingly practical, title "Home Economics."

HOMOPHOBE ⤷ *n*. Included here as an example of a deceptive use of a common word. This is normally taken to mean "one who has a hatred of homosexuals." In fact, the word means "one who *fears* homosexuals."

HONOR, DEBT OF ⤷ *n*. A gambling debt. Where the honor comes in is not entirely clear to the present author, but the phrase could be useful in the real-life situation of justifying to your spouse the necessity of paying a significant part of the household revenue to your bookmaker.

HUMAN ⤷ *adj*. It is odd indeed that the use of the word "human" in many modern contexts has in fact a dehumanizing effect on the subject under discussion. Thus, the term "human resources" as a synonym for "staff" somehow has the effect of placing the staff on the same level as "material resources," thereby making them as easily renewable or disposable.

HYGIENIC TREATMENT ⤷ *n*. Embalming.

⤷ I ⤶

I HEAR YOU ⤷ *phr*. Delightful, and extremely useful, Scottish expression meaning, "I don't agree with you, but I can't be bothered arguing with you." Of similar import, in the world of management, is "I'll take that on board."

ICON ∾ *n*. Once an icon was an idol – a depiction of a being of godlike standing. Now *everything*, whether divine, organic, or even inorganic, is an icon. A person may be described as an "icon in the municipal waste industry." (See also *job titles*.) Even the little symbols on my computer screen are icons. Don't overdo this one. The Beatles were an icon; Shakespeare was an icon; but you and I are not.

IDIOSYNCRASY ∾ *n*. Polite term for someone else's perceived weakness or failing, e.g., *shoplifting* (q.v.), variant sexuality, mania for collecting early adjustable wrenches, etc.

ILLNESS, GASTRIC ∾ *n*. Another euphemism-magnet, though many of the phrases used do convey a sense of good-humored revulsion at the memory of this unhappy experience. Here are just a few of these colorful expressions: Adriatic Tummy, the Aztec Two-Step, Bali Belly, Basra Belly, Delhi Belly, Gippy Tummy ("Gippy" from "Egyptian"), Hong Kong Dog, the Lagos Fox-Trot, Montezuma's Revenge, the Rangoon Runs, Spanish Tummy.

IMPROVEMENT ∾ *n*. A new commercial service that no one wants, introduced in order to justify a cost increase.

INAPPROPRIATELY REFERENCED MATERIAL ∾ *n*. Plagiarized material. I have heard this exquisitely euphemistic expression used in a radio interview by a university

chancellor, when referring to a scandal at his university involving the copying of
others' work.

INCIDENT ∾ *n.* An event of relatively little importance; a quickly passing minor event. Hence, widely used by the military to describe a horrific bombing in which much *collateral damage* (q.v.) is done, with many children maimed or killed. A "border incident" usually means that troops shot at each other across the border for a few days, and not many were killed. Interestingly, no one who has ever been shot at refers to their experience as an "incident." To hear your doctor talking about an "incident" may also be a matter of some concern, particularly if he is talking about a "cardiovascular incident," or a "cerebral incident," either of which may have much
the same significance as
an *episode* (q.v.).

INCLUSIVE LANGUAGE ∾ *n.* Avoiding the use of gender-specific pronouns, so as to avoid any suggestion of gender bias. Legislation commonly covers this by something of a cop-out – saying in the preamble that "he" includes "she" throughout. The present author once wrote a book on child development, and got around this problem by alternating the gender of his subject chapter by chapter; but this somehow failed to achieve a satisfactory result and, worse still, marred the elegant fluidity so characteristic of his prose style. His preferred option, where feasible, is to use the hitherto plural pronoun "they" in the singular sense, but the context of the sentence does not always permit this.

INDIVIDUAL BEHAVIOR ADJUSTMENT UNIT ∾ *n.*
A solitary confinement cell.

INFESTATE, TO ◦ *v.* Such a word does not exist, I hear you cry. But beware, the needless elongation of verbs is a disease that can spread like wildfire. At a medical conference not long ago, the author heard a distinguished medical expert talk about "burns that became infestated with maggots." In the otherwise excellent BBC program *Frost*, the leading character, a police inspector played by Sir David Jason, in speaking of local plans to put on a prestigious ball, uttered the line, "Denton is hardly ball orientated." And again, a vignette from the author's personal experience: overheard in a supermarket aisle, a visiting expert from the head office saying to the local staff, "This supermarket needs to do a better job of presentating itself."

INFORMED SOURCES ◦ *n.* Journalist's term meaning either "I've made this one up" or "I don't know where this came from, but it sure is interesting." My own informed sources, as hinted at in my preface, fall mainly in the latter category.

INSTIGATE, TO ◦ *v.* These days as often confused with "initiate" as "alternate" is with "alternative." But "instigate" has an altogether darker meaning. You initiate an action, but you instigate trouble, perhaps by fomenting unrest or dissatisfaction, or by setting in train a malicious plot. A government initiates a program of medical aid. Another government (not ours, of course) instigates an assassination plot.

INSURGENT ◦ *n.* Strictly speaking, a rebel, i.e., someone seeking to overthrow his government by force. Now, however, used to describe a person who resists the invasion of his country by a foreign power. This obviates the necessity of describing, for example, Iraqi "militants" (as they are also called) as "freedom fighters" or "the resistance" – terms that might be seen as giving them some legitimacy. The first Indian war of independence, in 1857, was for many years referred to by British historians (and in many cases still is) as the Indian "mutiny." A "counter-insurgency" is a military program to suppress resistance by "insurgents."

INTELLIGENCE ❧ *n*. (As in the "secret service") Not a euphemism at all, despite appearances. It's not just the spies telling you that they're really clever. "Intelligence" in this context means "information about what's going on," and did so long before it came to mean "cleverness" and to be measured by a "quotient" as the "IQ."

INTERACTIVE ❧ *adj*. This word does have a real meaning, but is often used as a flag word (see *paradigm*), in much the same way as its fellow flag word "proactive." So when you hear it used, be ready to interrupt. Ask: "When you say 'interactive' in this case, do you mean 'mutually interactive'?" This will at least stop the other person's flow momentarily, and with luck they will not notice your little tautology.

INTERIOR INTRUSION ENUNCIATORS ❧ *n*. These used to be called "burglar alarms."

INTERPRETIVE CENTER ❧ *n*. Nothing at all to do with interpretation or foreign languages. This is the modern name for a structure where information is on display for the public. The example most recently seen by the author, a wooden gazebo with panels displaying charts and photographs, was described on its street-front signage as a "Wader Bird Roosting Interpretive Center." In former times, this would have simply been called a "display," but "interpretation" is now evidently thought to be a more prestigious, or more intellectually distinguished activity.

INTERROGATION WITH PREJUDICE ❧ *n.* Torture.

INVASION, EUPHEMISMS FOR ❧ Insertion, incursion, intervention, police action, preemptive defense maneuver, interdiction (also used for "killing"), and cross-border deployment. Somewhere I have seen the term "vertical insertion" used for invasion by parachute. An invasive attack such as a heavy bombing raid may be called "surgical" to convey the impression that it is good for the patient, in this case the persons being bombed (sorry – I should have said "receiving air intervention").

INVENTORY ADJUSTMENT ❧ *n.* See this in an annual report, and you might like to consider selling your shares, since it often means "we now admit to the level of loss implicit in the inflated valuations previously ascribed to our assets."

INVOLUNTARY CONVERSION ❧ *n.* An airplane crash.

JOB TITLES ❧ A good deal of innocent amusement, and considerable *be*musement, may be derived from an inspection of the "Help Wanted" advertisements in the larger metropolitan dailies. The current fashion is to give jobs the most pretentious, and in some cases the longest, in others the most incomprehensible, titles. Here are a few culled at random from my recent reading:

Agrarian Assistant (a farmhand)

Business Development Representative (The accompanying job specifications made it abundantly clear that this was a simple sales position.)

Category Assistant

Cosmetologist

Culture and Change Manager (This ad informs us that "our client is a large, successful icon in the national energy market," so even icons apparently need "culture management.")

Facilities Manager (Given the various meanings attached to each of these words elsewhere in the world of job description, this one could be a toilet cleaner, or a school janitor, or the national manager of a chain of hotels!)

Full Retail Contestability Project Manager

Human Relations Officer (A "degree in Human Relations is required.")

Principal Project Officer, Public Space Service Coordination

Principal Workforce Capability Consultant

Relief Member Service Officer

Sexual Assault Coordinator (What does this person do?)

Spatial Analysis and Planning Advisor ("The Spatial Analysis and Planning Unit has a vacancy for an advisor to provide professional support within the Spatial Analysis and Planning Unit in achieving the effective translation of the Community and Corporate Plans into corporate support outcomes, medium/long term plans, policies and initiatives for the land use planning group.")

Spatial Knowledge Manager ("We are seeking a dynamic key resource with experience and dedication . . . and the ability to translate require-

ments into creditable and sustainable outcomes
for all stakeholders.")
Team Leader, Corporate Performance Management
Technology Auditor
Voice Operations Officer (At a university – the job
was that of a telephone receptionist.)

Even if we look only at the few examples quoted above,
questions present themselves. What, one wonders, could
a "degree in Human Relations" be like? What does the
"spatial analysis and planning advisor" actually *do*? Notice
that the "spatial knowledge manager" being sought is not
a person, but a "key resource." Are the responsibilities of
the "sexual assault coordinator" similar to those invoked
by the titling of a pamphlet issued to all staff within a
major federal government organization: "Sexual Harass-
ment – It's Everyone's Responsibility"? And it is not only
the job titles in these advertisements that are pretentious
or meaningless. The language within the body of each advertisement can offer some intriguing possibilities. Thus,
a lawyer is sought with a "proactive regulatory focus."

JUNIOR JUMPER ∾ *n.* Police slang for an underage
rapist.

JUST CAUSE ∾ *n.* Code name for the 1989 U.S. invasion of Panama. Planned under the name Blue Spoon,
the invasion and its preparations included elements of the
"Nifty Package," "Acid Gambit," "Blade Jewel," "Nimrod
Dancer," "Purple Storm," "Prayer Book,"
and "Sand Flea" plans.

JUSTIFY, TO ∾ *v.* To execute a person in pursuance of
a court order. A term out of use for some time now, but
in this age of euphemism watch out for its return.

❧ K ❧

KEISTER ❧ *n*. A box, trunk, or suitcase. But in common use (and I use the term "common" in both its senses), the anus. This latter use is thought to have originated through prisoners referring to the use of the anus as a temporary receptacle for valuable or contraband items. Somewhere in one of the many ridiculous books in the author's library (could it be the admirable *Anomalies and Curiosities of Medicine*, by Gould and Pyle?), there is the story of a patient presenting himself to a doctor with a carrot well and truly embedded in his keister. On being asked how it came to be there, the patient replied: "I tripped over it while gardening."

KEY COMPETENCIES ❧ *n*. Key skills. "Competencies" has largely taken over from "skills" now. After all, it's a much longer word.

KILL, TO ❧ *v*. Another euphemism-magnet. The rather endearing "whack" that has recently come to us in TV programs about the "mob" (the latter something of a euphemism in its own right, perhaps) may perhaps be forgiven, since it does not attempt to conceal that we are talking here about an act of malicious violence. But what about "account for," "bump off," "cleanse" (as in "ethnic cleansing"), "erase," "look after," "mop up," "take care of," "take out," "terminate," "carry out the final solution," "subject to maximum demotion," "top," and "waste"? And, in the military world, what about "render combat-ineffective"? Evasions, all of them. It is not by accident that the terms universally used for official killings of criminals – "capital punishment" and "execution" – contain no purely philological hint as to their meaning (other

48

than the fact that "capital" comes from "caput," or head, and hence could be argued to relate to the long outdated practice of beheading). It is noteworthy that in recent years terrorists have taken to referring to their murders of hostages as "executions," thereby seeking to give them the cachet of official action. "Executive action" has been used to refer to the assassination of a leader in a foreign country. And the wholesale murder of a political opposition is called a "purge," a term formerly confined to a medicinal treatment designed to cause evacuation of the bowels.

KISS THE DOG, TO ∿ *v.* To pick a person's pocket while standing face to face with him. For further information, the reader is referred to Eddie Joseph's *How to Pick Pockets* – another item in the author's collection of ridiculous books – for some remarkable revelations of just what is possible for an expert "dip."

Kiss the Dog

KITCHEN-SINKING ❧ *v.* In the world of accountancy, "kitchen-sinking" is what is happening when accountants exaggerate certain elements in the accounts of a business (i.e., by throwing in "everything but the kitchen sink"), to allow the current and future performance of management to be seen in a better light.

KNOWLEDGE, A LITTLE... ❧ *phr.* How often do we hear, as a supposed quotation, the words "a little knowledge is a dangerous thing"? Let's get this one right. Pope's actual words were:

> A little learning is a dangerous thing
> Drink deep, or taste not the Pierian spring
> There shallow draughts intoxicate the brain
> And drinking largely sobers us again.

The Pierian spring? This sprang from the ground at the point on Mount Pieria where a hoof of the flying horse Pegasus struck the earth. The liquid gushing out in response to the Pegasian hoof was the "blushful hippo-crene" mentioned by Keats (from *hippos*, or horse). Bore your friends silly with this one, and, if one of them calls out "sproingggg!" when you are talking about a spring springing up, *decimate* (q.v.) his body parts.

❧ L ❧

LANDSCAPED ❧ *v.* A term from real estate, but in-cluded in this book because of its metaphorical use as a synonym for "massaged" or "doctored." "We've landscaped the accounts a little, of course, Chairman, for public presentation purposes."

LAY OUT IN LAVENDER, TO ∾ *v*. To flatten, knock out, or kill someone who has annoyed you.

LEARNING CURVE ∾ *n*. Increasingly common cliché for use in interviews, when on the defensive. "Well then, Mr. Fernberd, tell us what you know about the mechanics of handling insurance claims in the professional indemnity area." "Well, of course I'd need to go through something of a learning curve on the job in that particular area – I'm looking forward very much to that. . . ."

LEGACY ADMISSION ∾ *n*. The admission to a U.S. college of academically inferior students because they are the children of former graduates.

LEVERAGE ∾ *n*. Another cliché that is becoming more and more common, and gradually replacing the now somewhat passé "mileage." "It's agreed then? If we put Purflight and Harbison on a retainer we'll get more leverage out of having their contacts with the Serbian market?" "Will we get more leverage with our high-end client base by giving them complimentary copies of the works of this man Bowler?"

LIBERATE, TO ∾ *v*. In Beethoven's time, to liberate was, for example, to release a political prisoner from prison. Now the term has been appropriated by those who are looking for a more acceptable expression for "invade and conquer." Can also mean simply "to steal."

LIFE ∾ *n*. (As in the term "life insurance") Death. The ultimate euphemism.

LIFE PRESERVER ∾ *n*. An old-fashioned word for a cosh, i.e., a small weighted bludgeon or blackjack – certainly not an instrument designed for the preservation of life.

LIFETIME GUARANTEE or WARRANTY ∾ *n*. A claim increasingly common in the marketing of objects and services. Just today I have seen, in a kitchenware shop, a frying pan carrying the legend "Lifetime Non-Stick Warranty." Ask the sales *consultant* (q.v.) who is boasting about a product's "lifetime guarantee" this question: "Whose lifetime – mine or yours?" There will be a moment of blank incomprehension, an expression indicative of wheels turning within a mind under pressure, then the reply: "No, it means the lifetime of the product or service." Now just think for a moment about what this means. It means that if the product falls apart, or fails to function, after six months, or if the service fails to be supplied after six months, the lifetime of the product or service has expired – and with it the guarantee. Always insist on a written explanation of exactly what the consultant's much-vaunted "lifetime guarantee" means.

LINEAR THINKING ∾ *n*. A term of contempt, sometimes applied to the thinking of the great Isaac Newton by chaos theory groupies and by other starry-eyed physicists manqués, all being people themselves totally unable to calculate the mathematics of planetary motion, discover the nature of colored light, invent the reflecting telescope, calculate the effect of gravity on the tides (never having seen the ocean, I might add), and invent differential calculus on a wet weekend. The term is often used in conjunction with an assertion that "Newton, of course, did not know about relativity" – a remark that could be made only by those who have not read Newton's *Principia*.

LIQUIDITY INTERVAL ∾ *n*. See *cash flow episode*.

LITTLE FELLER ∾ *n*. Sounds like an expression of endearment directed at your loveable little nephew, doesn't it? In fact, this was the code name devised for a series of four nuclear bomb tests carried out in July 1962 in Nevada.

Little Feller

LIVE ∾ *adj*. As an adjective, used to denote that a performance, a speech, a game of football, a war, etc. is being broadcast or telecast to listeners or viewers *as it takes place*. Or, as we would say now, "in real time." (What kind of time is unreal?) So far, so good. But increasingly we are told that what we are being played, or shown, is a "live recording." Yet this is an oxymoron. By definition, no recording can be live. What is meant in such cases is that the performance, speech, game of football, or war was recorded as it happened in some public arena, not in a studio with retakes and adjustment of frequency levels and so on. So let's not have this nonsense about "live recordings."

LOGISTICS ∾ *n.* Until recently, this has had only one meaning – the management of the supply and movement of necessary military equipment and manpower. But such a technical, even quasi-scientific, term was begging to be taken over for the purpose of aggrandizing much more mundane enterprises. So now it can simply mean transporting anything by truck. As evidenced by such signs as that seen recently on the back of a refrigerated truck, no doubt carrying meat or some other type of perishable: "Thompson's Cold Logistics."

LONG WORDS ∾ In a book about deceptive language, I admit to having promulgated, in several previous books, with tongue firmly in cheek, the notion that long and unknown words may be used to deceive (or, at least, impress) others. I now wish to redress the balance by claiming that the use of long words is per se by no means inimical to plain English. All of us use long words every day. Even sports commentators use long words, and I have recently heard them talk, among other things, of Roger Federer's "comprehensive self-analysis," of an athlete's "incomprehensible form reversal," of "the impossibility of ever beating the U.S. at baseball," of "the culmination of four years' hard work" by a kayaker, of the "unconventional preparation" of a baseball team, of the "aura of invincibility of a football team," and of a cyclist "controversially drafted into the team." Now these are all very long words – "comprehensive," "incomprehensible," "impossibility," "unconventional," "invincibility," and "controversially" – but nobody has the slightest doubt as to their meaning. The real enemy of plain English is what this book is about – the use of fashionable words and cant phrases, used solely to impress, or to substitute for the precise expression of meaning. The use of euphemisms to obscure or conceal the true nature of what is being talked about, to alter our perception of reality and to dull our moral sensitivity, is what concerns me and is the subject (and object) of this book.

LOOP ∾ *n*. (As "in the. . ." or "out of the. . .") Being in the loop implies that you know what everyone else in the loop knows. But loops are circular, and remember, if your driveway is circular you won't be able to get your car out. So if you're not in the loop, you might know a lot of stuff that the people in the loop don't know. For that matter, you could be "thinking outside the box," which is generally considered a good thing. Though, speaking personally, I'd like to think that I'd thought of everything inside the box before I started thinking outside it. I could go on writing about this forever, but it's time for me to "push the envelope" – possibly after conducting a "helicopter audit" (or overall appraisal, as we used to call it).
By the way, how can an envelope be *pushed*?

LOVER ∾ *n*. Just watch this word go the way of "gay." A lover used to be someone who loves someone else. Now it increasingly means someone who has a satisfying sexual encounter with someone else, the latter being not a "loved one," but a "trick" (itself previously confined to the meaning "a prostitute's customer," but now sadly widening its coverage).

LOW-COST DELIVERY PLATFORM, A ❧ *n.* (a) The Internet when used as a venue for banking transactions, thereby allowing banks to "downsize" their establishments. (b) A term from, you guessed it, the literature of nuclear weapons, referring to the potential of certain airplanes as alternatives to missiles for the delivery of these weapons.

LOW-YIELD NUCLEAR WEAPONS ❧ *n.* A really smart one, this. The use of the word "yield," with all its connotations of giving, surrendering, offering peace, etc., gives the impression that the person on the receiving end of one of these weapons is being given some kind of benefit.

❧ M ❧

MALADJUSTED ❧ *adj.* Misbehaving young people used to be called "naughty," "mischievous," or in the worse cases "juvenile delinquents." The changeover to "maladjusted" carries with it the implication that the failings of the young person concerned are due to a failure on the part of society to subject them to the appropriate adjustment, not to any personal flaws in their own personalities or their parents. "Maladjusted," however, has now fallen out of favor and is being replaced with a host of alternative euphemisms. The young persons in question may now be described as "difficult," as "overactive," as "underachievers," or as suffering from Attention Deficit Disorder (ADD), Hyperactivity Syndrome (HS), Attention Deficit Hyperactivity Disorder (ADHD), Oppositional Defiant Disorder (OPD), Cerebellar Development Delay (CDD), or Bipolar Disorder (BD). In the relevant medical literature, differential diagnosis within this general area does not seem to matter nearly as much as inventiveness in nomenclature and its accompanying acronymics. The danger in developing all this seemingly clinical terminology for conditions that apparently carry no biological identifiers, with the well-meant intention of justifying antisocial behavior on the part of the young, is that genuinely sad and life-destroying conditions such as full-blown autism – the extreme form of Autistic Spectrum Disorder (ASD) or Asperger's Syndrome (AS) – can be seen as less serious than they really are. Especially when one sees seventeen-year-old naturopaths on TV glibly declaring that "of course, Beethoven had Asperger's."

MANAGE, TO ∾ *v.* To *massage* (q.v.) or even suppress altogether news or information that you deem undesirable for others to hear.

MARBLE ORCHARD ∾ *n.* A cemetery.

MARGINALIZED ∾ *adj.* On the outer edge of society, as for example a group deprived of full participation in society by their poverty, their race, their religion, etc. Here the addition of "-ized" to "marginal" converts a factual statement to a blame-allocating statement.

MASSAGE, TO ∾ *v.* In the world of corporate and government euphemism, this can be assumed to mean "twist" or "distort." "If we massage the figures a little, we can show the desired outcomes." "Let's just massage that phrase from Lincoln's speech so it looks as though he was in favor of what we're going to do." Alternatively, "doctor." Both words may come in handy when referring to "financial engineering," i.e., false accounting or "cooking the books." This author once heard a senior partner in one of the big six accounting firms ask his client, in all seriousness, whether the client would like the accounts written up to show a profit of a million dollars or a loss of a million dollars.

MATRIX ❧ *n*. People are *still* using this pretentious word as a means of impressing others. It simply means "table," so why not *say* "table"?

MEET YOUR MAKER, TO ❧ *v*. Another synonym for "die." A friend of the author spent his declining years in a home for old people who needed care because of their disabilities. His was Parkinson's disease, which required help getting out of bed every morning. The home was run by a religious organization, and one of its younger nurses, full of religious enthusiasm, would greet him on these matutinal occasions with a merry "Well, Mr. W., are you ready to meet your maker today?"

MEMORIAL COUNSELOR ❧ *n*. A seller of grave plots in some American cemeteries.

MESSAGE ❧ *n*. A TV commercial. After all, no one in that medium is ever going to announce a commercial break by saying, "I'll be back after this advertisement," are they?

MICKEY MOUSE ❧ *n*. I like this one. A code name given by those supposedly humorless people, the Germans, to a 1944 commando operation that seized the Hungarian leader Horthy and set up a puppet regime.

MISSION STATEMENT ❧ *n*. A term already covered in one of the previous Superior Person's books, but well

worth another volley. How could the presumably hard heads that run big business ever have been seduced into adopting on such a universal scale this fashionable, pretentious term for something as ordinary as a set of objectives? Can it be, perhaps, that the highly paid executives of our corporations are not all that bright? What, after all, is a "mission"? Perhaps, it is a fervent proselytizing religious campaign, or a passionate dedication to some higher cause? Something of the stature of Luther's crusade to reform the church, or Wilberforce's to abolish slavery? No. It's generally a smug, self-congratulatory list of imagined virtues pinned to the wall of a bank for its customers to read while cooling their heels in line. When I become chairman of the board of a major company (offers may be sent to me care of the publisher), its mission statement will read in its entirety:
"To make bags of money."

MOTION DISCOMFORT BAG ∾ *n.* A bag for plane passengers to vomit into. The mild concept of "discomfort" obviates the necessity to refer to such an off-putting idea as "air sickness." Also known, in more direct fashion, as a "barf bag."

MUNICIPAL FARM ∾ *n.* Local jail.

MUTINY ∾ *n.* See *insurgent*.

MYTHICAL ∾ *adj.* Not to be confused with "legendary," since "mythical" refers exclusively to events that are fictional and "legendary" to events that, whether fictional or factual, have become widely revered and celebrated over time. A distinction evidently not known to the writer of the text for a boxed set of CDs sighted by your author recently, a reissued complete recording of Mussorgsky's opera *Boris Goudounov*, which is promoted on the cover as being "Boris Christoff's mythical recording."

∾ N ∾

NATIONAL ∾ *adj*. A good all-purpose euphemism, since "national" has connotations of "all-embracing," "wide-ranging," "patriotic," and the like. Hence used in political party names the world over, often with no regard to the particular policies of the party in question. Thus, in Australia the "Country Party," which existed to push the needs of the rural community, changed its name to the "National Party"; in the U.K. the right-wing lunatic fringe party called itself the "National Front"; and – the ultimate in meaninglessness – near the author's home town a small local agricultural show has changed its name to, simply, the "National."

NATURAL ∾ *adj*. Another good all-purpose euphemism. We are accustomed to thinking that if it's natural, it's *ipso facto* good. A perfect term therefore for, say, "alternative" medicines – and a more meaningful one incidentally, too, since "alternative" tells you nothing about what something is, only about what it's not. Oddly enough, "alternative" medicine is also often described as "complementary" medicine – frequently in the same health shop signage – though the two meanings are incompatible. If it's complementary, it's not an alternative to conventional medicine; it's a complement, i.e., an addition to conventional medicine. Unless, of course, it's *holistic* (q.v.).

NECKLACE, TO ❧ *v*. To murder someone by setting fire to a rubber car tire that has been secured around their neck. A "necktie party" is a lynching.

NEGATIVE ❧ *adj*. Ironically, the word – which is itself the ultimate expression of denial and subtraction, the very opposite of "positive" – is often used to soften the impact of an unpleasant reality. Thus, "negative growth" or "negative profit" somehow seem rather less unpleasant in accounting statements than "decline" or "loss" would be. "Negative containment" has a very specific meaning: a leak of radioactivity from a nuclear reactor. And did you know that there are "negative stakeholders." What are these? People, perhaps, who do not hold shares in General Motors?

NEIGHBORHOOD CONNECTION ❧ *n*. No, not an instance of suburban social networking across the fence on a Saturday afternoon. Your "neighborhood connection" is your local fence, i.e., a receiver of stolen property.

NETWORK ❧ *v*. This was originally a noun, meaning, in the words of Dr. Johnson's beautiful definition, "anything reticulated or decussated, with interstices between the intersections." Now, a verb requiring an even more complicated definition. To network is to maximize one's range of acquaintances, especially those from whom some form of benefit may be drawn, by constant and diligent communication with an ever-widening circle of persons. "We really must go to the faculty soirée, Natalie; there'll be so many opportunities in the room for me to reticulate and decussate, with interstices between the intersections."

NEWS UPDATE ∿ *n.* When a "news update" is announced on your TV, be not deceived. These are *never* updates. They are invariably repeats of the headlines from the last main newscast. If a genuine update is to be given, it is announced as "breaking news."

NIXON ∿ *n.* A poor-quality drug that has been passed off as genuine quality. Named, rather cruelly, after Richard M. Nixon, thus opening up for the rest of us an interesting new field of word-smithing – the use of ex-presidents' (and for that matter current presidents') names as slang for some object or activity that is thought to be evocative of their particular foibles. Do not write me with your suggestions.

NOMINAL ∿ *adj.* When said of a fee, beware. If the inducement for a service is that "the fee is purely nominal," always respond that, since the fee is only nominal, you assume that there will be no need to actually pay it.

NORMALIZATION or NORMING ∿ *n.* The mathematical massaging of test results to ensure that those whose results are exceptionally poor, or exceptionally good, are brought back towards the average.

NOT MATERIALLY AFFECTED ∿ *adj.* Commerce-speak for "adversely affected."

NUMBERS, DECEPTIVE ∿ What we normally think of as words are not the only deceptive form of language. There are also numbers. Indeed, when you think of it, numbers are adjectives. Despite the mistaken belief of many pure mathematicians that numbers are *things*, numbers exist only to tell you something about nouns, just as adjectives do, and therefore can be treated as words. A form of linguistic deceit that has been around for so long that we all take it for granted, and to that extent need all the more to be on our guard against it, is the use of misleading numbers in the pricing of goods. Yes, I'm talking about the familiar fact that shops, gas stations, publishers, and indeed most retailers price their goods not in whole dollars but in one or five cents less than the whole dollar figure. Thus, a $10 purchase is never priced at $10; it is priced at $9.95, or $9.99. Despite the fact that we would all tell ourselves that we are so used to this that it doesn't really affect us, the psychology of it remains intensely powerful. When we see the $9.95 price tag, our all-powerful subconscious mind sees only the $9. When we see a $24,999 price on a car, our subconscious mind does not notice the $999; it really sees the price as $24,000.

O

OBLONG ∾ *n*. Defined by Webster as "a figure having greater length than breadth." One of the author's favorite words, but one that is dying out, and being replaced almost entirely by its near-synonym "rectangle." In 1930s Britain, someone conducted a questionnaire survey of Anglican clergymen; the findings revealed that only a minority believed in the virgin birth or the resurrection. Asked to describe God, one of the respondents wrote that he thought of God as "a kind of oblong blur." A word that is included in this book as an example of a good, old-fashioned word that surely is safe from any of the twisting and corrupting attentions of the managers and the politicians and all the other cant merchants. Help the author in his campaign to revive it. Use it twice a week.

OCCUPATIONAL ❧ *adj*. Sometimes used to downplay the level of injury or disease that a worker is exposed to by his job. Thus, the radiation experienced by someone working with a nuclear reactor may be described as "only the standard occupational level." Once they start saying that it's only *nominal* (q.v.), beware.

OFFSHOREABLE ❧ *adj*. Able to be consigned, with a cost-effective outcome, to an overseas *facility* (q.v.). As, for example, the employment of human beings.

OPERATIONAL DIFFICULTIES ❧ *n*. Publicly stated reason for some act of incompetence on the part of an airline, a communications provider, a public utility, etc. The intended implication is that some event totally beyond the control of any reasonable human being has caused this service failure. A variant is "network difficulties," as used by London Underground officials to explain to passengers the delays caused by the July 2005 bombings.

OPERATIVE ❧ *n*. Like *consultant* (q.v.), a term used to conceal the true nature of an employee's work, in the hope that the element of prestige thus conferred upon his job title will reconcile him more readily to his relatively low wage. In general, "operatives" rank below "consultants" in the social pecking order. After all, consultants sell you something. An operative, on the other hand, drives a *resource recovery vehicle* (q.v.), or, in the case of a "traffic facilitation operative," acts as flagman at a roadwork site. A "cleansing operative" is a road sweeper. Basically, "operative" is replacing "worker," the latter being increasingly considered as too *infra dig* a word for our super-sensitive age. Note too that there is a subtle difference between "operative" and "operator." The "-or" ending tells you that the operator does something – he operates a machine, for example – whereas the "-ive" ending implies something a little more abstract, such as the supposed possession of organizational capacity. A keyboard operator is what used to be called a typist, whereas a keyboard operative is someone who might do other things that merely have some vague relation to keyboards.

OPTIMIZE/OPTIMAL ∿ *v.* and *adj.* Increasingly used as though they mean the same as "maximize/maximum." Get this right: "optimal" means "best"; "maximum" means "biggest." (The biggest is not always the best!)

ORDNANCE SUCCESS ∿ *n.* The degree of destructiveness of a nuclear bomb. "Ordnance" used to be the word for all kinds of weapons and armory. Increasingly it has come to be associated with the particular kind of weapon that no one wants to talk about directly.

ORGANIC ∿ *adj.* This usually means "of or pertaining to animals and plants," but in chemistry it can mean "containing carbon as an essential ingredient." This confuses the issue nicely when it comes to the common practice of describing farm produce as "organic." It is hard to imagine a fruit or vegetable or cut of meat as being *in*organic but, as we know, the use of the term "organic" by the vendors of these commodities is intended to convey that the commodities in question have been grown without exposure to chemical pesticide and fertilizers. In a world of ambiguities and euphemisms and confusing terminology, would it not be better to simply describe the produce as being "free from chemicals." But wait a minute, they're *not* free from chemicals; they're *composed* of chemical elements.

OUT OF THE MAINSTREAM ∾ *adj*. Not to be taken
seriously. A polite way to patronize the other person's
opinions or achievements, or for that matter
the other person himself.

OUTSOURCE, TO ∾ *v*. When a corporate or government agency outsources a task (i.e., pays someone outside
its own organization – often a *consultant* [q.v.] – to do it),
this may be happening because the task is too hard for the
agency itself, but – and this is much more likely – it may be
happening because the agency doesn't want to carry the
responsibility for the task's quality or outcome or because
an outside supplier can provide the service more quickly,
inexpensively, or accurately. There should be more out-
sourcing in private life. "Sorry, dear, I've outsourced the
cooking this month. Where will you take me
for dinner tonight?"

Outsource

OVERQUALIFIED ∾ *adj*. As in: "Well, Mr. Sopworthy,
we've been most impressed by your application, and you

certainly have impressive qualifications; indeed, the reason we won't be shortlisting you at this stage is that we feel you are in fact overqualified for the position." This is, of course, Olympic-class deceitful language. There is, in fact, no such thing as being overqualified for a job. While on the subject of a supposed surfeit of qualifications, let me share with you the salient points of James Murray's amazing letter of application for a position at the British Museum Library in 1866. (Murray did not get the job, but he did go on to greater things, in that he oversaw the monumental task of managing the writing of the *Oxford English Dictionary*.) My source for the following is Simon Winchester's admirable book *The Meaning of Everything*.

I possess a general acquaintance with the languages and literature of the Aryan and Syro-Arabic classes . . . with several I have a more intimate acquaintance as with the Romance tongues, Italian, French, Catalan, Spanish, Latin and in a less degree Portuguese, Vaudois, Provençal and various dialects. In the Teutonic branch, I am tolerably familiar with Dutch . . . Flemish, German and Danish. In Anglo-Saxon and Mœso-Gothic my studies have been much closer. . . . I know a little of the Celtic and am at present engaged with the Sclavonic, having obtained a useful knowledge of Russian . . . the Persian, Achæmenian Cuneiform and Sanscrit branches I know for the purposes of Comparative Philology. I have sufficient knowledge of Hebrew and Syriac to read at sight the Old Testament and Peshito; to a less degree I know Aramaic, Arabic, Coptic and Phenecian. . . .

There were giants in the earth in those days.

OWNERSHIP ∾ *n.* Very much in vogue as a modern managerial expression. Staff who are responsible for a certain area of an organization's work are said to "own" it. This is supposed to give them a feeling of empowerment, but note that it also helps absolve their superiors from responsibility when something goes wrong. School students are said to be given "ownership" of the subject matter or skills they are supposed to be learning. Related to "ownership" is the widespread use of "stakeholder" as a vague term meaning "anyone who could be said to have any interest in the matter." The world of social welfare trying to pretend that it is the world of hard-headed business.

∽ P ∽

PACIFY, TO ∽ *v*. To conquer by force of arms and keep in subjection.

PAINT THE TAPE, TO ∽ *v*. To falsify financial details so as to give a rosier picture of a deal being promoted.

PARADIGM ∽ *n*. A cant word from the world of academia. Certainly, it has a meaning – a classic example or pattern – but now it is used, only too frequently, not to convey that specific meaning but as a flag – a verbal flag inserted in a sentence to tell you that the speaker has intellectual (or managerial) credentials. Will we ever see this one drop out of favor with the highbrows manqués? Not, I suspect, until we have a "paradigm shift." You can always do your bit to return this word to the shadows from which it has crept into the sunlight by saying, whenever someone else has just used it in conversation: "Ah, paradigm – that's still in fashion, is it? Did you know that according to Webster its real meaning is 'an ordered list or table of all the inflected forms of a word or class of words, as of a particular declension or conjugation'? Or – wait a minute – was that the sense in which you were using it?"

PAYLOAD ∾ *n*. The amount of explosive material in the bombs carried by a plane. The human knee-jerk reaction to the word "pay" makes the idea of a "payload" seem almost beneficial.

PEACE ∾ *n*. War. As in the code name given by the U.S. Air Force to identify programs involving the provision of military equipment and training to overseas countries. The "British peace," or, as it was better known in its Latin form, the "*Pax Britannica*," referred to the maintenance by Britain of its forceful subjugation of other countries as members of its Empire. The term harks back to the simi-lar "*Pax Romana*," which lasted a good deal longer and did not leave behind quite so many intractable hostilities.

PEACEMAKER ∾ *n*. The decidedly unpeaceful Colt .45 handgun.

Peacemaker

PERFORMANCE ART ∾ *n*. A public display of the peculiar talents of one who would not ordinarily be regarded as either a performer or an artist. If the piece of performance art in question is entirely *extempore*, it may be called a "happening."

PERMANENT ∾ *adj*. Can often mean "temporary," and "temporary" can often mean "permanent." It all depends on what kind of ambivalent message the writer or speaker wants to give the public. "Setbacks," for example, are always described as "temporary setbacks." As are "difficulties" being experienced in war, in business, in international negotiations, etc., etc. The writer recently saw in his local paper a report that the municipal council was giving thought to the possibility of making the temporary restrictions on householders' use of water "permanent for the time being."

PERPETUAL CARE FUND ∾ *n*. An extra fee charged by a cemetery for giving the client a guarantee that the deceased's grave will be well-maintained in perpetuity. In this case, the phrase "in perpetuity" may merit the same degree of skepticism as the phrase *lifetime guarantee* (q.v.).

PERSONALITY, A ∾ *n*. A person who is highly paid to make frequent appearances on television, but who cannot truthfully be described as an actor, a singer, or a comedian. Such a person may also be called a "celebrity."

PERSONNEL ∾ *n*. There is something dehumanizing and impersonal about this term for people, and this makes it a useful aid in sugaring the pill when staff layoffs are being talked about. "Some rationalization in personnel levels" somehow makes it seem as though it is statistical entities that are being talked about, not human beings. Thus, in military language, an "anti-personnel mine" or an "anti-personnel bomb" somehow doesn't sound like something designed to hurl shrapnel into the limbs and abdomen of a human being; rather the implication is that some kind of collective material resource is the target. In business, by the way, the "cleansing personnel" are the cleaners.

PERSONNEL CEILING COMPRESSIONS ∾ *n*. Job cuts.

PIGMY GRAND ∾ *n*. Not a modern euphemism, but included here as a classic example of the tendency, mentioned elsewhere, for human beings to use words to aggrandize the nature of their institution, their product, their job, etc. Around 1910, the Gramophone Company put out the first ever hornless gramophone. It was made small and cheap, to fill a gap in the market, and they decided to call it the "Pigmy." But by the time it came to be advertised, it was being called the "Pigmy Grand." Anyone who has seen one of these machines will fully appreciate that "grand" is not a word any reasonable person would ordinarily associate with it.

PING-PONGING ∾ *v*. Delightful euphemism discovered by the author in one of his more eccentric reading forays. A process in which a number of medical specialists refer a wealthy patient to one another in succession.

POINT OF ORDER ∾ *n*. A disputed point of procedure in meetings. Everyone knows this, but when is a point of order *not* a point of order? The answer is to be found in Hansard for the House of Commons in the United Kingdom for 7 April 1970. Yes, this is the kind of thing that your author cuts out and retains for years and years.

Mr. Speaker: Order. That is a bogus point of order.

Sir W. Bromley-Davenport: On a point of order. We continue in the House to get this cheating on the other side. (Interruption.) When have I raised a point of order that was not a point of order, you great, ugly brute?

Mr. Speaker: Order. I must remind the hon. and gallant gentleman that I am neither great nor ugly.

Sir W. Bromley-Davenport: I apologize, Mr. Speaker, if that was thought to be a reflection on the Chair. But we look at these animals on the other side of the House day in and day out. We cannot particularize.

My point of order is quite simple, short and fair. Within the last twenty minutes we have had one moron, the right hon. Gentleman – if I may say so; he is not right and he is not honorable. (*Hon. Members:* "Which one?") Now we have another one.

Mr. Speaker: The hon. and gallant Member must –

Sir W. Bromley-Davenport: Mr. Speaker, I will withdraw that.

Within the space of ten minutes we had another one, with spectacles on his kisser to try to make himself look more intelligent, who raised another point of order which was not a point of order. When, Mr. Speaker, will you regard this as cheating? (*Interruption.*) I am not raising a point of order. I am raising a point of order on points of order which are not points of order.

Mr. Speaker: Order. Points of order on points of order that are not points of order are not points of order.

POLICE ACTION ∾ *n*. Undeclared war. As for example the Korean War.

POLITICAL CHANGE ∾ *n*. Henry Kissinger's phrase for the defeat of the U.S. in Vietnam.

POOR, THE, EUPHEMISMS FOR ∾ It used to be said that "the poor are always with us." This may be true in the sense that, if poverty is defined, as it usually is by social scientists, in terms of the lowest x% of the income distribution, there will always be people within that x%, even in the most affluent populations. But in terms of the language used to describe poverty, the poor are no longer with us. The squeamishness that has prevented us from talking about the handicapped or the disabled has also prevented us from calling the poor "the poor." Instead we have the "lower socioeconomic group," the "underprivileged," or even the "negatively privileged." The latter somehow rather wondrously conveys that the poor are actually privileged – just not as privileged as others. A similar kind of squeamishness has governed the terms introduced over the last half century for poor countries. Instead of being called "poor countries," they came to be called "underdeveloped," but even that was considered to be potentially hurtful to the countries concerned, and so they have come to be called "developing," a term that avoids the original meaning entirely and in no way distinguishes them from wealthy countries, which, after all, are always developing, and generally on a larger scale and at a faster rate. Sometimes "developing" countries are called "less developed," and I have even seen them referred to as "the lesser (*sic*) developed." Poor countries are also sometimes called "industrializing" or "third world" countries, which somehow conceals the intended meaning to an even greater extent. Why do we perennially suffer this compulsion to cloud the very meaning of the language we speak and write, out of this passion for *niceness*?

POPEYE ∾ *n*. Code name for a U.S. campaign of rain-making during the Vietnam war, under which planes seeded clouds over Laos with silver iodide, with the intention of bringing about heavy rain on the Ho Chi Minh Trail, thereby disrupting the North Vietnamese supply line.

POPULATION TRANSFER ∾ *n*. Compulsory perma-nent evacuation of residents for resettlement somewhere else. Feasible only in totalitarian states, those natural seedbeds of euphemism.

PORKY ∾ *n*. A lie. From the rhyming slang "pork pie." The untruth told by your enemy is a "flagrant lie." The little white lie that you yourself are occasionally obliged to tell, from the very best of motives, may be jocularly referred to as "one of my little porkies."

POSTMODERN ∾ *adj*. Another "flag" word, normally used not to convey a meaning but rather to flag the writer's "with-it-ness." The latter, I should explain, is a term currently in favor with your author as part of his much-derided campaign to return the Anglo-Saxon ele-ment to preeminence, or, as your author would say, "over-strengthness," in our language. Yes, while others talk of "postmodern," I talk of "premodern." The poet Samuel Rogers, whose poems are still anthologized but totally forgettable, once said: "Every time a new book comes out, I make a point of reading an old one." Them's my colors. When anyone says "postmodern" in your hearing, ask with instant enthusiasm: "Wow! Postmodern! Does

that mean, like, futuristic?" Then watch them stumble
and ultimately withdraw in confusion when
they try to define the term.

POWERPOINT ⚬ *n.* A computer program designed to
help the slow-witted make a "presentation" to an even
more slow-witted audience. The term is doubtless derived
from the name Jack Point, the professional fool in
the operetta *The Yeomen of the Guard*.

PREGNANCY ⚬ *n.* A euphemism-magnet of the high-
est order. Everyone is familiar with the genteel "expect-
ing," but were you aware of the brilliantly conceived (if
you'll pardon the word "conceived") "infanticipating"?
Then there are:

> awaiting – or its fuller version awaiting the patter of
>   little feet
> bay window, having a
> broody, clucky, or on the nest
> bun in the oven, to have a
> club, in the
> delicate way, in a
> eating for two
> family way, in the
> Irish toothache, having an
> lady in waiting
> waiting woman, a

Or terms such as "gravid" or "enceinte" may be used –
terms that are straight-out synonyms for "pregnant" and
not intrinsically euphemistic at all but that, because they
are relatively uncommon and therefore less plain-spoken,
may achieve the desired degree of delicate
obliquity in polite conversation.

PRE-ORDER ∽ *v.* Does this mean anything different from "order"? After all, if it did mean something different, surely there would exist the corresponding term "post-order," in other words an order lodged after the object ordered was delivered.

PRE-ORGASMIC ∽ *adj.* Frigid (said of a woman). A term from the wonderland of American psychotherapy.

PRE-OWNED ∽ *adj.* Secondhand, used. Usually said of motor cars, but can be found in any area of the second-hand goods trade. Thought to lessen the degree of shame involved on the part of the purchaser in not purchasing new, and thereby make the prospect of a secondhand purchase more attractive. Other versions are "previously owned" and even simply "owned." A trawl through the language of the classified advertisements in your local newspaper may provide some intriguing phrases, especially since the need for brevity in such advertisements gives rise to some interesting ambiguities. One is the highly ambiguous phrase "little use," by which the advertiser means "not used very much – really, for all intents and purposes as good as new," but which can equally be read as meaning "not much use to anyone."

PREVENTIVE ∽ *adj.* As in "preventive war," "preventive detention," "preventive action." All of which seek to take the high ground over some ethically questionable act by using a term that in other contexts is unexceptionable – "preventive medicine," for example.

PROACTIVE ∽ *adj.* Ah, the language of "management team" meetings! Those of you who are obliged to take part in these meetings, make the experience less stupefying by taking notes in which you score the speakers for the number of times they use the basic clichés of the genre: "down the track," "proactive," "outside the box," "pushing the envelope," "fast-track," "the bottom line," "at the end of the day," and so on. Your assiduous note taking will be observed, and you will be earmarked for promotion. Just a few of the many other classic management clichés to watch out for are:

best practice
ball park
big picture
box/square, out of the
core (as in undertakings/business/promises/objec-
    tives, etc.)
extra yard, mile, etc., going the
fast track
game plan (a highly regarded staff member may be
    spoken of as "one of the best players in the *team*
    [q.v.]")
goalposts, moving the
heads-up
helicopter audit
loop (q.v.), in the/out of the
mover and shaker
outcome-oriented/focused/driven
result-driven/focused/oriented
revisit
touch base with
value added
win-win

PRODUCT ∾ *n*. A product is, of course, something produced, such as this book. You have "a product" or "the
product." But there is a growing tendency among the

euphemizers to equate "product" (used without the definite or the indefinite article) with "outcome." Thus unproductive people such as accountants and bankers can talk about their "product upturns" or their "product forecasts."

PROGRESSIVE ∾ *adj*. Quality of one's own thinking, in contradistinction to the other person's, which may be described as regressive. In Tasmania in the late twentieth century, there was a trend for "progress associations" to be established, with the aim of modernizing aspects of Tasmanian society. This, rather delightfully, led to the establishment of "regress associations" by those for whom "progress" in itself was not necessarily a good thing. Some concern on the part of the these founders of regress associations may have been understandable, since "progressive" is a term much in favor with totalitarian governments to characterize policies, such as *reeducation* (q.v.), property resumptions, and *population transfers* (q.v.), which impact harshly on some of their citizens.

PROPOSITION SELLING ∾ *n*. Not so much a deceptive piece of language as a deceptive way of using language. This rather wonderful term refers to a common high-pressure sales technique. The salesman puts to you a series of propositions so worded that you have no option but to agree with them. "Well, Mr. Forbet, you'd agree wouldn't you that having more money in the bank is better than having less? Yes? And you'd like to have more money in the bank than you've got now? Of course. Now, wouldn't you agree that a product that costs nothing and is guaranteed for life is worth having? . . ." And so on, until he springs on you the one supposed link between all these self-evident propositions and the dubious claims for the product he is selling.

PROTECT, TO ᜈ *v*. A word, with its derivatives, to be wary of when it comes your way. We all know what a "protection" racket is in the world of urban crime. In the era of imperial expansion, the term meant much the same thing. Thus, the establishment of a "protectorate" in theory offered a small and powerless country a powerful country's protection against its foes, but in reality conferred on it the status of colony. For a "protection agency" in a totalitarian regime, read "secret police."

PROTECTIVE CUSTODY ᜈ *n*. A word that can hide a multitude of sins. Generally, the person being taken into protective custody is not the one being protected. In the 1930s, the German equivalent was used to describe detention in a concentration camp. The term "concentration camp" itself is a euphemism, in that the word "concentration" when allied with the word "camp" would, before it lost its philological virginity, have implied little more than a bringing together of campers in close proximity, and thus could have been used to describe a happy lakeside summer camp for children.

PROVERBS ᜈ Thought to contain the wisdom of the ages, but often deceitful in the extreme, as anyone who has read Charles Lamb's list of fallacious proverbs will agree. They include:

A bully is always a coward.
Cheats never prosper.
Never look a gift horse in the mouth.
Enough is as good as a feast.
Love me, love my dog.

To these I might add the following examples of my own – all being proverbs the truthfulness of which I view with grave suspicion:

A friend in need is a friend indeed.
All roads lead to Rome.
All things come to him who waits.
An apple a day keeps the doctor away.
Ask and you shall receive.
Barking dogs seldom bite.
Early to bed and early to rise makes a man healthy,
    wealthy, and wise.
Hard work never killed anyone.
He who hesitates is lost.
It is better to give than to receive.
Take care of the pence, and the pounds will take
    care of themselves.
More haste, less speed.
See a pin and pick it up, and all the day you'll have
    good luck.
Slow and steady wins the race.
The more things change, the more they remain the
    same.
Waste not, want not.
Where there's a will there's a way.

PROVOCATION ∾ *n.* What weak small countries invariably do to big powerful countries to force the latter,
    much against their will, to invade them (sorry –
            I should say *pacify* [q.v] them).

PROXIMITY TALKS ∾ *n.* A somewhat delicate piece of
diplomacy-speak. When two countries are in disagreement
and not talking to each other – perhaps even have broken
off diplomatic relations – then a third country that remains
in close contact with both may act as an intermediary to
enable some exchange of views to continue. In the
domestic arena, perhaps, the term could be brought into

use when neither sister will talk to the other over the issue of bathroom time, but each will talk to the brother.

PUBLIC SECTOR BORROWING REQUIREMENT  *n.* A reference to this in a government financial report is a sure sign that the said government has been, or will be, spending more than it can afford on something.

PURIFICATION  *n.* Said of documents, means much the same as *sanitizing* (q.v.). Said of government actions affecting people, at its worst means "ethnic cleansing" (see *kill*) or the extermination of the unwanted under Stalin and Hitler.

PUT DOWN, TO  *v.* To kill an animal, especially a pet. In particular, a horse that has broken a leg during a race or show-jumping competition. There would perhaps be fewer equine "put downs" in the world if the established convention was that the person riding the horse at the time should be put down as well.

PUT IN ORDER, TO  *v.* To massage and doctor, for example, a file, until it is thoroughly "purified."

 Q

QUALIFICATION  *n.* Given its overtones of "quality" and "certification," it is not surprising to find this to be the word of choice for accountants wishing to state, without drawing too much attention to the matter, that there is something unusual about this year's accounts.

QUANTITATIVELY CHALLENGED ∾ *adj*. Fat. Seen in a U.S. paper on the problem of child obesity. Odd that it should be used in this exact sense, since one would think its natural meaning would be "thin," as a euphemism for anorexic.

QUARANTINE ∾ *n*. Euphemism for a military blockade. Also, when used as a verb by public relations people, to keep a particularly controversial problem or issue "in the back room," i.e., not a factor for public consideration. (The original "quarantine" was the forty-day period allowed to a newly widowed woman to live in her late husband's house.)

QUESTION, TO ∾ *v*. To be "questioned by the police" is a halfway stage between "being wanted by the police to help with their enquiries" and "being charged." The term "to verbal," referring to the supposed practice of police to report, as if true, imaginary confessions said to have been made by arrested men during interview, is an odd usage, since such confessions are by mouth and therefore the term should surely be "to oral."

QUID PRO QUO ∾ *v*. A *quid pro quo*, as everyone knows, is the good turn that is deserved by another for his good turn to you. "You scratch my back, and I'll scratch yours." But this author has seen it used as a verb in the *mission statement* (q.v.) of a consulting firm. Leafing through this statement (yes, it stretched to several pages), he came upon the capitalized words "Quid Pro Quoing" (*sic*), which at first glance he assumed to be the name of a village in Vietnam. Inspected more closely, decapitalized and hyphenated, the text read "We will cement client relations with fully integrated quid pro quo-ing practices."

❦ R ❧

RAINMAKER m *n.* One of the more delightful terms from the world of big business. A rainmaker is someone who, by virtue of his business connections, his reputation, his charm, his energy, or simply his relatives, has the power to attract money from investors or clients for new business. Often he is paid a "consultancy fee" to "network" with his contacts, or given a paid position on the board so that his name can be used to promote the venture – or, to use another business metaphor, to "raise the wind."
"Never mind your CEO or your chairman – does the board have a genuine rainmaker?"

RATIONALIZE, TO m *v.* Another bad thing to hear your boss talking about. In the world of managerial euphemism, we all know what "rationalize" means: there'll be job cuts.

REAL ESTATE, THE LANGUAGE OF m The true creative engine of the euphemism. As in the case of *death* (q.v.), a full listing would be endless. You know the sort of thing. The following are all examples sighted by the author himself in advertisements in his local newspapers and real estate agents' windows. In many of these cases, the author's translations reflect the impressions given by accompanying photographs.

Real Estate Language	*Translation*
Close to all facilities	noisy
Close to transport	school bus stop at front door
Cool	windy

Cozy	small
Fabulous	a fable
Family/eating area	no dining room
Great potential	needs internal walls, plumbing, and wiring
Home office	one of the bedrooms has been spoiled
Ideal for first-home buyers	you'll have to compromise on quality
Ideal investment	you can't get the tenants out
Leafy neighborhood	forest fire area
Like fine French wine	overrated and overpriced
More than meets the eye	no street, and even less interior appeal
Neat	tiny
Needs a little TLC	needs tender loving care *and* a new roof
Offers considered before auction	and used to work up the other bidders
Old-world charm	needs money for repairs and total updating
Open plan	drafts are a real problem and probably no walls
Price slashed	was way overpriced to begin with
Privacy from street	drive slopes down too steeply for your car
Quaint cottage	front door opens onto kitchen
Riverfront	floods after heavy rain
Room for pool	doesn't have pool
Secluded	the postman doesn't call this far out
Spacious	costly to clean

Starter or investment	a normal person would not want to live here
Ultra-modern	ghastly design
Unique	*really* odd
Unobstructed views	extremely windy

REAL ESTATE AGENT m *n*. The long-established use of the word "estate" for this job description is an example of a particularly early euphemism, since an estate is more than just a house on a suburban block – the word conjures up visions of rolling hills, a manor house, perhaps even a castle, an ornamental lake, herds of livestock grazing on ancestral lawns, and so forth. Similarly, "industrial estate" is now widely used to conceal the fact that the conglomeration of dirty, noisy, and ugly buildings on the edge of town is not a salubrious model center for industrial enterprises, created by a master designer. (If the industrial estate is not quite so noisy or dirty, but its design is particularly dehumanized, it may be called a "technology park.")

RECEIPTS, STRENGTHENING m *n*. Taxes, increasing. A U.S. economist's creation, this one.

RECEPTION CENTER m *n*. A strip-and-search room for incoming prisoners in a jail.

RECTIFICATION OF FRONTIERS m *n*. The seizure of territory by force of arms.

RED-FLAG WORDS m Certain words are used so often for purposes of deceit or pretension that, when encountered, they should affect the reader's mind like a suddenly erected red flag. These words say to us: "Watch out! Possible deceptive language ahead!" Here are just a few:

adjustment	challenge
consultant	deconstruction
develop	flexible
holistic	incident
matrix	nominal
paradigm	postmodern
preventive	rationalize
special	structure

REEDUCATION ∾ *n.* Mental reconditioning by a totalitarian regime. Used to be called "brainwashing," a term that seems to have gone out of currency lately, but could usefully be revived, in respect to both political and religious indoctrination.

Reception Center

REFORESTATION UNIT ∾ *n.* Some of my examples come to me, of necessity, through the assurances of a third party and not directly from a source that I have been able to check personally. This is such a one. I am assured that it has been used by a U.S. government agency. And its meaning? Would you believe . . . "tree"?

REGULARIZE ❦ *v.* To restrict in some way the person, property, or activity being "regularized." In one version, a country may "regularize" its relationship with another by invading it.

RELATIONSHIP ❦ *n.* A word that, in the age of the television soap opera, has increasingly become a synonym for interpersonal attachment. How often, during an episode of one of these "human interest" series, does one of the characters tell another that he or she wants to "talk about our relationship"? There are a host of words that then step forward to take their place in such a discussion. There may be something that one party wants to "share" with the other, or one may wish to express the feeling that they are "comfortable" with what the other is saying. Dammit, is it *compulsory* to have a "relationship" with someone? Can't we be just say that we're friends, or lovers, or enemies, or whatever? I'd be more comfortable with that, and you might be as well.

RELATIVE DEPRIVATION ❦ *n.* Poverty.

REPRESENTATIVE ❦ *n.* This used to mean, and in some quarters still does mean, one who represents a person or organization. Someone who speaks with appropriate authority on behalf of another. Increasingly, its meaning has come to teeter on the brink of "salesperson." Thus, a senior professor of cardiology representing a university medical faculty at an international conference may well be, in effect, a medical representative; but if someone at the conference has the words "Medical Representative" on his business card then you can be pretty sure that he is a traveling salesman for medical equipment or consumables. The part-time salespeople who live in your local suburb and who call at your home to take orders and to deliver the brand-named products of certain large retail businesses specializing in this kind of merchandizing are often called, not just "representatives," but various grades of representative. One of these grades, as sighted by the author on a business card, is that of "Presidential Representative."

REPRIVATIZATION ∾ *n*. A reduction in government support. A term once used by the Reagan administration in the U.S., referring to a policy of cutting back on the level of government support in certain sectors of economic and social policy. After all, what government would want to be seen to be "cutting back" when they could be seen instead to be "reprivatizing"?

RESORT ∾ *n*. A pleasure palace by the sea or in some other salubrious location, designed to house affluent vacationers. Consequently, the latest word of choice to describe an old people's home. (See also *facility*.) Today, I saw the following sign on such an institution: "Sir James Retirement and Care Resort." Dare I add that, inescapably hovering in the back of one's mind when seeing this usage, is the phrase "last resort"?

RESOURCE RECOVERY VEHICLE ∾ *n*. Trash collection truck or dumpster. The implicit message of this euphemism is that the truck is not just picking up trash to dispose of it at the dump (sorry – at the transit or transfer station), but rather is a sophisticated instrument for the redevelopment of society's resources. Probably driven by NASA technicians with higher degrees from MIT.

RESTORATIVE ART ∿ *n.* Funeral industry term for the beautification of corpses.

RESTORE ORDER, TO ∿ *v.* To subdue another country by force of arms and invasion.

RESTRUCTURE, TO ∿ *v.* To *massage* (q.v.) a report or other document in order to distort its message in your favor.

REVENUE ∿ *n.* It is not by accident that all the tax authorities in the English-speaking world refer to themselves not as "tax" but as "revenue" agencies. "Revenue" is a much friendlier word than "tax." Revenue is money that is received. Tax is money that is taken away. If there were an agency for the carrying out of state killings (gosh, there must be one in Texas, now that I think of it), it would probably be called a "Closure Department."

REVERSE ENGINEERING ∿ *n.* Taking apart a competitor's product to see how it works and then making your own version.

RIGHTSIZING ∿ *n.* See *rationalize.* They come up with a new one for job cuts every year. "Rightsizing" sounds so much friendlier than "downsizing."

RISK MANAGEMENT ∿ *n.* An interesting example of a term that was introduced into the world of business management for a very valid reason, but that has since lost its original meaning and acquired a lowest-common-denominator meaning instead. The original concept was that risks should be assessed with a view to striking the right balance between those that must be insured against, those that need not be insured against, and those that should be insured against only partly. Now "risk management" has become simply a synonym for "insurance."

ROLLING READJUSTMENT ∾ *n.* A two-word expression encountered in the writings of economics gurus who wish to talk about a depression without calling it that.

∾ S ∾

SANITARY WARDEN ∾ *n.* An "attendant," or, in plain English, a cleaner, in a public toilet.

SANITIZE, TO ∾ *v.* To remove potentially embarrassing content from a document that is to be made public.

Sanitize

SAVANT, AUTISTIC ∾ *n.* An example of the power of the media to cause change and confusion in the use of language through its love of euphemism. Since the film *Rain Man*, the term has been universally adopted in order to euphemize the previous crude but direct and colorful usage "idiot savant." This is unfortunate, since throughout history many "rain men" (people who perform amazing feats of calculation, memory, music, and so on) have in fact not displayed the typically autistic symptom – the intense level of introspection that precludes them from normal human relations – but rather have been people of very low intelligence, a different thing entirely. Incidentally, one of the common specialties of idiot/autistic savants is calendar calculation, i.e., almost instantly naming the day of the week for any given date from centuries past. For those who find this a magical ability, let me inform you that there is a mathematical formula that allows anyone to do this, though the calculation that takes the rain man a few seconds would take you a quarter of an hour using pen and paper.

SAVE, TO ✎ *v*. All too often, in commercial advertising this is a virtual synonym for "spend," since the saving being promoted can be achieved only by spending. "Buy three, and save three times as much!" (See also *free*.)

SECLUSION ✎ *n*. Solitary confinement in an *adjustment center* (q.v.).

SECTIONED ✎ *adj*. Locked up in the "booby hatch/ hutch," i.e., "madhouse" or "funny farm," against your will. A more dignified term is "mental health institution," but note that even this is a euphemism, since what is being talked about is really a mental *illness* institution.

SECURITY COORDINATOR ❧ *n.* A bodyguard.

SELF-ASSEMBLY ❧ *n.* A misleading term commonly affixed to furniture purchased from a shop specializing either in cheap mass-market discount goods or in high-end Scandinavian-design products. The term is misleading in two senses. First, its grammatical structure, in having the "self" as being the object of the "assembling," gives the entirely false impression that either (a) you are to assemble not the furniture but your own body or (b) the item of furniture will assemble itself by some robotic process. Secondly, if one accepts the apparently intended meaning, i.e., that the purchaser can assemble the product, extensive hands-on research over a significant part of the author's lifetime has conclusively demonstrated the falsity of this assertion.

Save

SELF-CONTRADICTIONS ❧ A special interest of the author in his capacity as collector of the curiosa of media English. The sports star who, having won his event, was seen on camera saying, with modest mien, that he felt "very proud, and at the same time very humble." The celebrity introduced at the start of the show as the "guest host." The bishop who commented on a preliminary decision about the proposed appointment of woman priests by saying that he was "both heartened and disappointed." The TV finance guru who predicted for a new product "a massive niche market." And the news reader who reported that the municipal authorities had decided "to make the water restrictions a permanent fixture for the time being." There is also the metaphor that is not so much mixed as mangled: commenting on the problem of drugs in sport, the champion swimmer was heard to say that "the tip of the iceberg is not here yet."

SELF-DELIVERANCE ❧ *n*. Planned suicide.

SEMIDETACHED ❧ *adj*. Not detached – as, one house from another. Originally the term was supposed to have had some validity, since it referred to a case where two houses were joined to each other by a common wall but not joined to any other house on the other side. Even so, it is doubtful whether anything could be sensibly said to be "semidetached" – a thing is either detached or attached. Now, however, one hears the term applied to rows of terrace houses that are certainly attached to others on both sides.

SHOPLIFTING ❧ *n*. A crime thought by many who perpetrate it, and even by many in society at large, to be not so much a crime as a sport – and not infrequently a team sport. ("Perpetrate," by the way, has only recently given us "perp" as a synonym for the person who commits a crime.) This quasi-tolerant approach to the practice on the part of so many has led to its attracting a number of relatively friendly euphemisms. Indeed, the word "lifting" itself implies that no crime is involved – merely a physical transfer of an object from one place to another. Shopkeepers therefore are ever keen to replace the term with "shopstealing"; and yet "shoplifting" still holds its own. Shoplifters may "boost," "divert," "drag," or "hoist" their booty rather than lift it. If they are more than mere amateurs, they may be equipped with "booster bloomers" or "hanger hooks" to assist them in secreting their acquisitions about their person. Those who conceal the "lifted" goods between their thighs are called, rather delightfully, "crotch walkers."

SHORT-ARM INSPECTION ∾ *n*. Military term for the inspection of naked soldiers for signs of venereal disease.

SIGNIFICANT OTHER ∾ *n*. In an age when people may be unmarried, married *de jure*, married *de facto*, divorced or divorcing, in a homosexual partnership, engaged, going steady, or in some other category in an ever-widening range of relationships, there has been an increasing need for an all-purpose term for the other person with whom someone is in a relationship, be it of whatever kind. For this purpose, "partner" has held the field for some time now. But, humans being humans, a more pretentious term had to be found, and here it is. Your partner has now become your "significant other."

SLUMBER ROOM ∾ *n*. The room in which a corpse (sorry, the "departed") is laid out by a funeral director in preparation for the funeral. Why not add a little spice to family *visitations* (q.v.) by eschewing the term "guest bedroom" in favor of this somewhat more ambiguous appellation?

SOCIAL OWNERSHIP ∾ *n.* Sounds less threatening than "nationalization," just as "restoration of choice" sounds better than "privatization."

SOCIAL SECURITY ∾ *n.* Income support, or entitlement to it. It is interesting that some terms that when first used involved the euphemistic distortion of meaning (what is "social" about income-supported security?) have over long currency acquired an accepted validity for their new meaning. Thus does language change. Let us just hope that "downsizing" never achieves the same acceptance.

SOCIALLY CONSCIOUS ACHIEVERS ∾ *n.* Beatniks who have deserted their youthful philosophy of life and achieved material success, but none the less still wish to be seen as standing tall morally.

SPECIAL ∾ *adj.* A *red-flag word* (q.v) if ever there was one. Like "protect," a word to be wary of, particularly if the nature of the specialty is unspecified. A convenient way for governments to conceal from the public the exact nature of an activity, or to minimize public concerns and pesky questions. Thus, "special branch," "special squad," "special processing," "special activities," and the like. Then there is its euphemistic use to disguise a reference to a deprived group, as in "special education."

SPEECHES ∾ It is when we are listening to the speeches of the high and mighty that we need to be particularly on our guard for deceptive language, since the words flow quickly past our mind with little opportunity for us to think, "Hey, wait a minute, what's that he said?" To illustrate this, let us take short excerpts from two famous speeches from an earlier, euphemism-free age, and translate them into the kind of thing that would have emerged today, had the speaker delegated the writing of the speech to his corporate affairs manager.

> *Winston Churchill:* We shall fight on the beaches, we shall fight on the landing grounds, we shall fight in the fields and in the streets, we shall fight in the hills; we shall never surrender. . . .

> *His corporate affairs manager:* Our game plan will be to enter upon an engagement, in which we shall conduct our operations in a variety of physical spaces – the peripheral, the non-urban, the council-approved thoroughfares, and the elevated con-figurations. We will at this time defer indefinitely consideration of the option of a negative win-win situation outcome. . . .

> *Abraham Lincoln:* That we here highly resolve that these dead shall not have died in vain, that this nation, under God, shall have a new birth of freedom, and that government of the people, by the people, for the people, shall not perish from the earth.

> *His corporate affairs manager:* That we here record a consensus that any collateral damage incurred during this exercise shall be not be classified as counterproductive, that this nation, under the respective belief systems of its demographic groupings, shall reinstate a best-practice, non-hierarchical power structure, and that, down the track, user-participatory teaming systems shall, in the end result, go forward.

SQUIRREL ∾ *n.* Psychiatrist. I like this one. A slang usage that I was unfamiliar with until very recently. The derivation is that the worthy practitioners of this art are said, with reprehensible disrespect, to "feed off nuts."

STAGFLATION ~ *n*. As a descriptor of the state of a country's economy, this doesn't sound too bad, does it? The "stag-," suggestive of "stagnation," after all suggests some degree of stability. The "-flation" could mean anything – deflation, inflation, reflation or whatever. Overall, not too alarming a term, wouldn't you say? I am, however, assured by my economist friends that a period of stagflation involves not only a stagnant economy but also rising inflation and high unemployment.

STAKEHOLDERS ~ *n*. See *ownership*.

STATE FARM ~ *n*. Local jail.

STRATEGIC REALIGNMENT OF FORCES ~ *n*. Retreat. A military term. Another with the same meaning is, believe it or not, "exfiltration."

STRUCTURAL SURPLUS ~ *n*. A loss. The kind of surplus that a business has when it has produced more goods than it can sell, so that its income does not match its expenditure.

STRUCTURE ~ *n*. A building, of course, or something put together from its parts; you know that. (But when used in academic articles. . . See *construct*.)

SUNSET INDUSTRY ~ *n*. The industry sector that provides services, such as special accommodation, for the "chronologically gifted," i.e., the elderly. (See also *twilight years*.)

SURVIVABILITY ◌ *n*. A nuclear-war term. The degree to which a country could survive a nuclear attack. Also the degree to which a politician could survive a political blunder. ("Deniability" would help here – see *credibility*.)

◌ T ◌

TAKE CARE OF, TO ◌ *v*. Another of those euphemisms for "to kill"; but also can mean "to bribe."

TAKING SHAPE ◌ *phr*. An intrinsically meaningless phrase used in the retail trade to avoid the direct description of customers' deficiencies. (See *accessible parking*.) A large department store visited from time to time by your author has a section of its women's fashions floor that specializes in clothing for the larger woman – or should we say the "fuller figure." For many years, this was named the "Big Is Beautiful" section. Recently, I observed that the "Big Is Beautiful" signs had been taken down and replaced with "Taking Shape" signs. In other words, a form of words that meant something has been replaced with a form of words that certainly does not mean what it is supposed to mean, and if it means anything at all actually means the opposite of what it is supposed to mean.

TEAM ◌ *n*. Formerly descriptive of a side of players in a team sporting event. Now often encountered as a propagandistic synonym for the downtrodden staff of an organization. Thus, the staff entrance of a department store is as likely to have "Team Entrance" on the door. The unsubtle implication intended to engage the minds of both passersby and the staff themselves is that the people who work in this store are a group of close-knit friends who are just having the time of their life working together to score high sales and happy customer outcomes. And yet . . . have you ever tried to get someone on the perfume counter to help you with a purchase at the footwear counter when the latter is unattended? Even when there is a sign saying, "Please see a team member for assistance." Of course, one of the implications of your being a "team member" rather than a "salesperson" or a "cleaner" or a "floor manager" is that it is much harder for the customer to work out what you actually do. By this means the naturally defensive mentality and evasive techniques of the government bureaucracy are adapted to the retail environment.

TECHNICAL ∾ *adj*. Adjective beloved of the stock market and other circles where unpleasant eventualities need to be sweetened for public consumption. A "technical adjustment," "technical correction," or "technical reaction" signifies that the market has "eased," i.e., fallen in the day's trading. In law, a little lapse from legality may be described as a "technical breach." And, in business management, a "technical loss" or a "technical downturn" is a loss or a downturn respectively. In short, "technical" may be used to mean "not real." *Nominal* (q.v) has much the same force.

TERMINATE, TO ∾ *v*. To end or finish something. A word that is a true pomposity-magnet. (See also *terminative patient outcome*.) I still remember with appalling clarity something that was said to me many years ago by an acquaintance who was at the time taking a higher degree in psychology. His work involved an experiment in which the experimental subjects' responses were triggered by the experimenter (i.e., my acquaintance) switching a light on and off. In describing this experiment to me, instead of saying that he switched the light off, he said that after each subject's response, he "terminated the light manually."

TERMINATIVE PATIENT OUTCOME ∾ *n.* Death. But "terminative patient outcome" looks better as a heading in the performance indicator statistics, doesn't it?

TERMINOLOGICAL INEXACTITUDE ∾ *n.* Just the tiniest, tiniest departure from the truth. Not really a lie, maybe just a little mistake, maybe just a marginally incorrect statement... Am I convincing you? Oddly enough, the originator of this expression is thought to have been the great Plain Speaker Winston Churchill, in a 1906 speech in the Commons. (See also *truth, being economical with the*.)

THEFT, EUPHEMISMS FOR ∾ Lifting. Liberating. Helping oneself to. Peculation. (See also *shoplifting*.)

THERAPEUTIC MISADVENTURE ∾ *n.* An *incident* (q.v.) in which a patient is given medical treatment that is either flawed or just plain wrong, with unfortunate consequences.

THINK TANK ∾ *n.* Selected from a *team* (q.v.) to think up work for a "task force" and subsequently an "implementation group." After the work of all of which is done, the boss decides that something else will happen. (See also *thought shower*.)

THIRD AGE, THE ∾ *n.* Oldies. The no-longer-working population. As in "the University of the Third Age." Is

there a fourth age? In my own case, I would hope so, but regrettably the evidence suggests this
not to be the case.

THOUGHT SHOWER ∾ *n.* Brainstorming. An invented term – thought up in a thought shower, no doubt – the intention being to avoid using "brainstorming," on the grounds that this could conceivably give offense to persons suffering from conditions, such as epilepsy, that entail electrical malfunctions in the brain.

Thought Shower

TITLES, TRENDY ∾ Titles can be not only pretentious (see *job titles*) but also trendy, and in the rush to express a fashionable, racy image, lose all their meaning. A national film and sound archive known to the author, which was called from the day of its establishment "the National Film and Sound Archive," not long ago decided to change its name to "Screensound." A change from a clear, precise, and meaningful title that made it entirely clear to the world exactly what this institution did, to a trendy, snazzy title that may have satisfied its managers' aspirations to "with-it-ness" (see *postmodern*) but that told next to nothing about the nature of the institution. Government and semi-government agencies, which hanker to be seen as dynamic private sector corporations, are especially susceptible to this kind of obfuscatory window-dressing.

TOLERANCE LEVEL, PENETRATION OF ∾ *n*. Heard in a TV interview with a big-name CEO from the retail industry. "One effect of higher oil prices is that the tolerance level of consumers has been penetrated." The author's tolerance level is penetrated repeatedly, though rarely in relation to movements in retail industry profitability.

TOTAL QUALITY MANAGEMENT ∾ *n*. Pretentious and sickeningly self-congratulatory term for a fashionable system of management, intended, for obvious reasons, to be foolproof, entailing the preparation of vast volumes of "best practice" paperwork the purpose of which is to remind managers of all the things they have to do. Usually introduced into a workplace by *outsourced* (q.v.) *consultants* (q.v.) who themselves have no managerial experience at all (but probably have degrees in "Business Administration") and are paid enormous sums of money for pulling this wool over the eyes of those who do. "Total quality assurance" is a supposedly reassuring indication to a firm's potential clients that it has put itself through this process.

TOUCH SIGNATURE ∾ *n*. A dactylogram, i.e., a fingerprint.

TRANSFER PRICING ∾ *n.* A reference to the need for some "transfer pricing" in the company chairman's oral report to the board might not attract undue attention. But transfer pricing is a form of accounting (see *creative*) in which costs incurred by one branch of a business are understated, and/or sales income overstated, in order to improve the overall tax position of the business as a whole.

TRANSIT POUCHES ∾ *n.* Military term for the containers in which the bodies of soldiers are brought home from the battlefront. Replaced the previous term "body bag," which, while disrespectful in its very crudity, was at least plain English. And what could be more demeaning to the fallen than the concept of their being shipped home in something as small and insignificant as a "pouch"? Also increasingly used for the same purpose are "transit cases" and "transit tubes," the latter calling up a particularly horrific image.

TRANSIT STATION ∾ *n.* (Alternatively, transfer station) I first saw this appellation on a sign pointing down a dirt road leading off a rural highway. How strange, I thought, that there should be a major bus interchange station way out here, and with such an unprepossessing road leading to it. It took me some time to realize that "transfer station" simply meant dump. A variant seen more recently is "domestic transfer station" – not a labor exchange for domestic servants but a dump for household rubbish.

TRIAGE ∾ *n.* This term has for years had an honorable place in the world of emergency care, and has meant the sorting of casualties by paramedics, for example at a large-scale traffic accident, in order to determine their relative priorities for treatment. So far, so good. Now, rather chillingly, it has also been adopted by the defense strategists of powerful countries to describe the sorting of lesser nations into those that, in the event of war, will be helped and those that will be left to succumb to their fate.

TRIANGULAR TRADE ∾ *n.* A form of the slave trade common in the eighteenth century, involving the import and export of goods between three different continents on each voyage, the central leg of the voyage being for the carriage of slaves.

TROUBLES, THE ∾ *n.* Bloody mayhem in Northern Ireland. A classic case of euphemism by understatement.

TRUTH, BEING ECONOMICAL WITH THE ∾ *v.* Not actually lying – no, just not quite conveying the full facts, maybe just pardonably letting slip from the mind one little aspect of the matter. An innocent omission from one's responses to the committee of inquiry. Not a breach of faith, or a failure to honor one's oath to tell the truth. An understandable lapse in comprehensiveness. (See also *terminological inexactitude*.)

TWENTY-FOUR-HOUR SERVICE ∾ *n.* (As for your newly purchased air conditioner, hot water system, etc.) A phrase worthy to stand alongside such classics as "the tooth fairy," "Father Christmas," and "lifetime warranty." On the only occasion when your author sought to avail himself of one of these services, in the hope that the noise his new ducted air conditioner system was making in the ceiling at 2 A.M. could be stopped, his phone call was taken by a recorded message that claimed that it would relay the call to the repairman in question. The latter's response came at 11 A.M. the following day.

TWILIGHT YEARS ∾ *n.* Commonly taken to refer to the last years of one's life, and hence a term to stand alongside those mentioned above under "aged." Thus, a "twilight home" is a hospice for the moribund. These days, the mileage (or should I say "leverage"?) extracted from this term by various comedians has all but extinguished its serious use. However, I am now proposing its revival, having in mind that "twilight" originally meant something much broader than its present meaning of the half-light experienced at sunset. In Elizabethan times, "twilight" meant the half-light not only at sunset but also at dawn. This earlier meaning is most beautifully illustrated in Marlowe's great poem "Hero and Leander," in the passage describing Hero's blushing appearance beside the bed in which she has lain with Leander, after her clothes have slipped from her:

> Thus near the bed she blushing stood upright,
> And from her countenance behold ye might
> A kind of twilight break, which through the hair,
> As from an orient cloud, glimpse here and there,
> And round about the chamber this false morn
> Brought forth the day before the day was born.

Ah, Marlowe. What would he have written if he'd lived as long as Shakespeare?

∾ U ∾

UNACCEPTABLE ∾ *adj.* The official term for the level of damage that, in a nuclear attack, would guarantee the defeat of your country.

UN-AMERICAN / UN-AUSTRALIAN / UN-[*any nationality*] ∾ *adj*. Not virtuous. The ultimate expression of national holier-than-thou-ishness.

UNCERTAIN ∾ *adj*. Description, for public information purposes, of a future outcome (as of a military or business venture) that is expected to be very, very bad.

UNCOLLECTED WRITINGS OF [*writer's name*] ∾ *n*. Collected writings. As in the title of a book containing a previously unpublished collection of writings by that author.

UNEMPLOYED, EUPHEMISMS FOR ∾ A person without a job may be "between jobs," "resting," "self-employed," "working on a change of life," "taking stock," "studying the classifieds," "looking around," "working at home," or "enjoying a break."

UNFORESEEN GEOLOGICAL EVENT ∾ *n*. Term used by a tunneling company in its media releases about what the rest of us would call a "cave-in," when a tunnel it was building beneath a suburban housing complex collapses.

UNILATERAL ∾ *adj*. What you call an act or decision by another country, agency, or person if the act or decision in question is one that you don't approve of and haven't agreed to. A polite way to save face when admitting defeat. Thus, the Rhodesian Declaration of Independence in the late 1960s had the word "Unilateral" tacked onto it by the British so that they could still talk about it without looking silly.

URBAN RENEWAL ∾ *n.* The destruction of perfectly serviceable downtown neighborhoods and the attendant dispersal of the poor to an *uncertain* (q.v.) future so the developers can, with state approval, appropriate the land and begin their next profit-making projects.

∾ V ∾

VEHICLE SIGNS, PERPLEXING ∾ "Partial Zero Emission" (seen by the author on a municipal council truck). (See also *resource recovery vehicle.*)

VENEREAL DISEASE ∾ *n.* Syphilis was once known in polite circles as "blood disease," "bone-ache," "the hazard of the town," or "the French disease." In nineteenth-century England, it was necessary to have euphemisms for the condition, since 10 percent of adult males had it. To have gonorrhea was "to have blue bells"; I am unable to explain this. The use of the term "French disease" reflects a tendency on the part of the British to attribute to the French the origins of all British weaknesses and deficiencies. Thus, a soldier who deserts has taken "French leave," the implication being that French soldiers are notoriously given to unauthorized retreat from the field of battle. In the Edwardian era, British pornographic photographs were sold from under the counter as "French pictures." The French, needless to say, have a similar approach to the use of the word "*anglais*," as in "*le vice anglais*," i.e., homosexuality.

VERBING ∾ The fashionable trend in recent times to make a verb out of a noun. Thus, we take the noun "access" and use it as a verb ("you can access our friendly website at any time"). Other recently verbed nouns have included "pressure," "monster," "*ease*" (q.v.), "sequence," "gift," "*necklace*" (q.v.), "network," and "process." (In a recent sitcom episode I heard a character who had just broken some disturbing news to another say, "You may need a little time to process this.") Your author admits to some ambivalence as to whether this is a bad thing. Language must change and expand, and this is one way in which it does. The problem is that in the process there can be ugliness and, more importantly for the purpose of this book, ambiguity and confusion. Next time you hear one of these function-changing neologisms, ask yourself whether it was a necessary one. Often there's an existing verb that serves the purpose equally well.

VERTICAL TRANSPORTATION UNIT ∾ *n*. Elevator or lift. A term said by my sources to have been used within no less an agency than the state department of a mighty country.

VISION STATEMENT ∾ *n*. Most would think that it is enough – indeed more than enough – for a corporation to have a *mission statement* (q.v.). But there are no bounds to the innocent enthusiasms of those within corporations who have a passion for the codification of the self-evident. For them a mission statement is not enough. There must also be a vision statement. Of course the term "vision" has connotations of a higher level of perception. We are intended to see the corporation as a kind of enlightened being, gazing into the distant future in a trancelike state of virtue and heightened perception. But which comes first, the mission or the vision? And how can the statements be worded, by the public relations people who write them, in such a way as to be different in content without being mutually inconsistent? A certain amount of innocent pleasure can be derived from comparing the two statements for any one organization, noting the points of duplication and inconsistency, and drawing attention to these at the front counter.

As an example of the extremities to which corporations and associations may be driven by the worship of the grandiose statement of purpose, I have in front of me a document published some years ago by a state-funded cultural council in Australia. (And remember that Australians are generally thought of as being plain-spoken.) Page 8 gives a statement of the council's "Vision." Page 9 gives the council's "Mission." Pages 10 and 11 list its "Principles." Page 14 is a list of its "Objectives." Appendix A lists the ten achievements of the council for the year just finished. Of these ten "achievements," six, i.e., the majority, are that the council:

> developed its philosophy
> established and explored its mission
> engaged in wide-ranging consultation
> nurtured a policy development process
> crafted seven principles
> formulated a strategic plan

VISITATION ∾ *n.* A special word for a very special kind of visit – the kind in which a supervisory or monitory person, or group of people, visits an institution to inspect it or certify it or investigate it (perhaps even to conduct a "helicopter audit" of it). However, given the trend for needless lengthening of verbs (see *infestate*), we can bet our boots that before long the word "visit" will disappear completely and when we go to see our parents on Sunday we will be paying them a "visitation."

VOLUNTARY SEPARATION ⮂ *n.* Resignation, usually of an involuntary nature in the wake of a *restructure* (q.v.).

⮂ W ⮂

WAITPERSON ⮂ *n.* If it really was so important not to differentiate between the male and the female in this area, why not just call them all "waiters"? A sign in a restaurant saying "Please take a seat and your waitperson will be with you shortly" gives me the inescapable impression that there are special staff called "waitpersons" whose function, as Milton put it, is to "only stand and wait." Curiously enough, this is what many of them seem to do. But, harking back to the first issue, why should people not be differentiated by gender? After all, we still use the terms "Mr.," "Mrs.," and "Ms."

WAR CRIMINALS ⮂ *n.* The other side.

WASTE-RECYCLING RECEPTACLE ⮂ *n.* A trash bin.

WEEKLY ⮂ *adj.* Monthly. How can this be, you ask? My example comes from a 300-page women's monthly magazine published in Australia – the *Australian Women's Weekly*. Long, long ago, long before most of you were born, but not of course before I was born, the *Australian Women's Weekly* was a tabloid-format weekly. When a decision was made to convert it to a monthly, it was decided to leave its name unchanged, no doubt to ensure that its entire existing readership was not lost overnight. When the change was made, it was even rumored that some of the magazine's faithful readers continued to buy and read it every week, not noticing that the content remained the same in every four successive issues. Thus do the requirements of commercial branding change our language so that a word may mean something totally in conflict with its true meaning.

WHEN THE FAT LADY SINGS ∾ *phr.* Another one for the management team meeting (see *proactive*) as an alternative to "at the end of the day." Frequently used at sporting events as in "It's not over until the fat lady sings."

WHITE LIE WARD ∾ *n.* In a military hospital, the ward for soldiers whose injuries are so severe that they are not expected to survive.

WINE LANGUAGE ∾ Ah, the flights of meaningless metaphor engendered by the wine trade! In the vain attempt to describe in objective terms the gustatory qualities of different wines, connoisseurs of the "blushful hippocrene" (see *knowledge, a little*) have developed a language newer than Esperanto and even more mystifying. Fine shades of taste being just as indescribable in words as colors are, merchants have resorted to the language of three-dimensional geometry, architecture, and mechanical physics to convey some hint of their meaning. Thus, the wine list on the table at my club today included wines that were "well rounded," "full bodied," and "elegantly structured." The elegantly structured wine also had a "complex palate." On the principle of "set a thief to catch a thief," it is perhaps time now for wine language to undergo, at the hands of a French professor of philosophy, the celebrated process of deconstruction. But don't start me on "deconstruction" here – see instead the excellent David R. Godine edition of *The Superior Person's Third Book of Well-Bred Words*, page 20. Failing that, the time could be ripe for the Peter Bowler Taxonomy of Wine Descriptors, by which wine is categorized according to whether it "kind of tastes like lemonade, but sourer and without the fizz," "tastes sort of like grape juice with a bit of vinegar in it and looks red," or any one of a range of even subtler descriptors that are much too elegantly structured and full bodied to go into at length here. In the meantime, here are some further examples of the qualities that can be attributed to wines, in contemporary wine language:

 A wine can *be*:
  beautifully balanced, with elegance and length
  almost unbelievably tight
  hollow
  wild and unfettered
  tight and firm
  hard
  clean
  empty
  soft
  long and precise
  flat
  spotlessly clean and tightly focused
  gently grippy
  tight, wiry, and focused, with finesse and poise
  pure, taut, and frisky, with an impressive depth
   and drive
  generously proportioned
  clever,
  or
  a trifle simple

 A wine can *have*:
  a beautifully balanced structure
  a steely taut structure
  great intensity and finesse (two qualities, by the

way, that would ordinarily be regarded as
  mutually incompatible)
loads of attack and length
a linear style
a bony spine
a supple texture and a calm, elegant sense of
  harmony
a tightly structured, ultra-clean finish
a well integrated, finely structured texture
a struck-flint character
understated intensity
marvelous focus, structure, and length
a seamless texture
power and structure
plenty of weight and reasonable length
broadness
a round framework
or
profundity

A restaurant advertisement in the newsletter of a major southern-hemisphere university has this to say about a recommended Shiraz: "an exotic bouquet of blackberries and other sweet fruits is followed by a full-bodied, powerful, rich red with great purity, and a blockbuster finish that lasts."

In his search of the wine literature for the above examples, the author must admit that he found two that delighted him and that should become models for the genre in the future. One wine was described as having "absolute slurpability," another as being "livelier than a sack full of ferrets."

WIRELESS ∾ *n*. Operating without wires, needless to say. Included in this book for no better reason than to express the author's delight at its present-day revival. In his childhood, which readers may suppose to have been a long, long time ago, what we now refer to as a "radio" was invariably referred to as a "wireless," and this naturally became the term invariably used by the author in adult life. This was a cause of great hilarity on the part of his children who, whenever he referred to a program as being "on the wireless," would be reduced to helpless laughter. "Dad's using one of his old-fogey words!" was the usual comment. Now, at last, "wireless" has come into its own. First, there came the "wireless link" between TV sets in adjacent rooms, permitting the clandestine duplication of access to Pay-TV. Now, we have all manner of references to "wireless" facilities in the world of digital access to the Internet, email, broadband, etc., etc. "What goes around, comes around," the author would say, were it not for the fact that this itself has now become another old-fogey expression.

WOMYN ❧ *n*. Women. Another invented word, the intention here being to remove the seemingly sexist inclusion of the word "men" in the word for women.

Philologically, there is no basis for this concern.

Womyn

WORD PROCESSING ✢ *n*. Just possibly the very first piece of computer language to suck us, kicking and screaming, into this strange new world. At the time it seemed a pretentious and inhuman term to replace "typing," but ever since then no one has been able to think of a better. Can it be that there are some management terms that are *not* in fact deceptive? There are, of course, plenty of deceptive computer and telecommunications terms. To stop my computer, I have to click on "Start." To turn on my wife's mobile phone, she has to press a little button that says "No."

∽ X ∽

X-RAY AUDITING ✢ *n*. Self-congratulatory term used by auditors and corporations as an assurance that financial records are "transparent." In terms of actual auditing procedures, it has no specific meaning.

X-WORD, THE ✢ For "x," substitute whatever letter commences the particular word that is thought too indelicate for speech – or, in some cases, even for writing down. Thus, the "f-word" for "fuck." The "n-word" for "nuclear." The "f-word" for "fat." The "c-word" for "cancer." And so on. In an author's case, the "r-word" for "remaindering."

XYLOPHONE TREATMENT, THE ✢ *n*. In public relations, a process applied to a proposed public statement during a final vetting to ensure that all the relevant points have been made and that they have been made as powerfully as possible. "Have you given it the xylophone treatment? Does it hammer all the tone-bars?"

∞ Y ∞

YEARS YOUNG ∾ *phr.* As in "he's eighty years young." Insincere and patronizing way to refer to the age of your friends and relatives.

YOU-ORIENTED ∾ *adj.* Another gem from a mission statement – this time a bank's. "You, the customer, are our focus. Our team of front-end consultants (*sic*) is totally you-oriented."

YOUTH CENTER/YOUTH GUIDANCE CENTER ∾ *n.* A detention and punishment center for young criminals. The intended implication is that this is a social welfare and vocational education center.

∞ Z ∞

ZAUBERFLÖTE ∾ *n.* Many of you probably think that this is a delightful fairy-tale opera by Mozart, known in English as *The Magic Flute*. A common mistake. It was in fact the German army's code name for a savage 1943 campaign to find and kill the members of the partisan resistance in Byelorussia.

ZIGZAG PRINCIPLE ∾ *n.* In business, the unplanned development of a venture by trial and error, i.e., going this way and that, as circumstance compels.

A Note on the Type

The Superior Person's Field Guide has been set in Matthew Carter's Galliard, a type introduced by the Mergenthaler Linotype Company in 1978 under the direction of Mike Parker. A type designer of impeccable pedigree and formidable knowledge, Carter took on the challenge of interpreting a French sixteenth-century face for the then-new medium of phototypesetting, christening it with the name Robert Granjon applied to a type he first cut about 1570. At the time Carter started work on his new type, Granjon's work was little recognized among designers; his italics had been co-opted as partners for the Garamond types and his romans heavily reworked under the name Plantin. Rather than attempt a literal copy of a particular type, Carter sought to capture the spirit of a Granjon original, and in so doing created a type with a distinct heft and a dense color on the page, and a sparkle not found in most Garamond revivals.

Design and composition by Carl W. Scarbrough